A
Renewable Resource Economy

by
Robert D. Hamrin

PRAEGER

PRAEGER SPECIAL STUDIES • PRAEGER SCIENTIFIC

New York • Philadelphia • Eastbourne, UK
Toronto • Hong Kong • Tokyo • Sydney

Library of Congress Cataloging in Publication Data

Hamrin, Robert D.
   A renewable resource economy.

   Includes bibliographical references and index.
   1. Renewable natural resources—Government policy—
United States.   2. Conservation of natural resources—
Government policy—United States.   I. Title.
HC103.7.H25   1983   333.7   83-17820
ISBN 0-03-063753-8 (alk. paper)

**To My Parents, Charles and Violet,
in their Golden Anniversary year,
My love and deep gratitude**

Published in 1983 by Praeger Publishers
CBS Educational and Professional Publishing
a Division of CBS Inc.
521 Fifth Avenue, New York, NY 10175 USA

© 1983 by Praeger Publishers

456789   052   98765432

Printed in the United States of America
on acid-free paper

FOREWORD

Russell W. Peterson

"It is safe to say that the prosperity of our people depends directly on the energy and intelligence with which our natural resources are used. It is equally clear that these resources are the final basis of national power and perpetuity."

With this quote from President Theodore Roosevelt, Dr. Robert Hamrin begins in Chapter 1 of this important volume to demonstrate to us the critical need to undertake a new course in our country and, indeed, in the economic and environmental affairs of the world. He ably chronicles how we, as a nation, have lost sight of the profound insight expressed by President Roosevelt early in this century, an insight which many others, including some of the finest economic thinkers of both earlier times and our own times, have shared.

Hamrin consciously and, in my view, properly emphasizes the United States, though this problem clearly has a global dimension. Our nation is large and powerful, is very energy and resource intensive, and has a material standard of living that is admired by many around the world. Yet, even though we have a strong conservation tradition, in many key ways we are a wasteful society. While Americans support a conservation ethic and often carry it out in their personal lives, our society is structured so that decisions are made that do not reflect certain fundamental realities; for example, the finite limits of nonrenewable resources such as fossil fuels and minerals, or the promise offered by more extensive reliance on our key renewable resource—the energy of the sun. Hamrin shows us the reasons for the incomplete basis for our society's unbalanced decisions, and provides many concrete examples to put meat on the weak, conceptual bones. In the process, he provides ample practical rebuttal to the current crop of Pollyannas who ignore both the constraints and opportunities of the real world of land and water, sun and air, plants and minerals.

But Hamrin does more than provide us with understanding and knowledge. He defines a way to fuse the insights of economics with the insights of ecology to create what he terms a "bioeconomics" for the future. This is a major contribution to the way we should think about many practical issues on our nation's current agenda and, if adopted, would bring major advances in both the near and long term. Significantly, Hamrin does not ignore but rather emphasizes the positive impact of bioeconomics on such topics as unemployment, urban problems, and others which are not often seen as linked to environmental and resource issues.

As I mentioned, there is a global facet to the problems dealt with by Hamrin, which has been termed "the global problematique" by the prestigious Club of Rome. In my opinion, one of the major issues of our time is whether legitimate human needs and aspirations can be met around the world. The only possible solution is through the pursuit of sustainable development. Hamrin correctly points out that if the United States pursues this goal in our own country, our leadership and economic importance in the world will dramatically assist others around the world to do the same. If this does not occur globally, serious consequences lie ahead, not least of which is an increased probability of armed conflict between nations in competition for the shrinking amounts of traditional economic resources.

Dr. Hamrin is well qualified to undertake this ambitious and significant work. Solid academic training and experience have been followed by front-line experience as an economist with both the congressional and executive branches of the federal government, including work with the President's Commission for a National Agenda for the Eighties. I commend this volume to people from all walks of life who have a concern for the type of nation and world they will leave for their children and grandchildren.

July 1983

PREFACE

This book was born out of a growing conviction that it is high time to reconcile our approaches to the economy and nature. Since the first critical step in any process of reconciliation is communication, the purpose of this book is to open one channel of communication between economists and environmentalists in the hope of demonstrating that the two communities really share a great deal in common.

Put simply, the environmental-conservationist camp has not wanted to be bothered with consideration of such matters as job losses or productivity declines, while the economics-business camp has most often dismissed what they perceive as the doomsday warnings of resource depletion and pollution overload. As is often the case, it seems so much easier to position oneself at the end of a spectrum rather than to plunge into the murky gray area where nasty and complex problems usually abide, challenging all purist perspectives. The facts are that jobs are lost due to pollution controls and productivity is lost when people get sick from unhealthy air and water.

It is time to start bridging the gap between these two artificially separate worlds. It is not enough, as some are prone to do, to simply say that the market will take care of things or that people's vast ingenuity will always see us through. This is naive optimism, neglecting the harsh reality that nature does impose irreversibilities that no amount of human ingenuity is going to restore. Consider, for instance, the hundreds of species that have become extinct in this century.

How does one begin to bridge the gap? Undoubtedly, there are many approaches one can take. I have chosen a fairly direct route in the form of a three-part message. Part I deals with the facts — the realities of both the physical world and the economic world. In both spheres, the attempt was made to present the facts as they are, not as we would wish them to be. The data come from a wide variety of sources that in most cases have no axe to grind.

In the second part, the fun really begins. It starts with a journey through the history of economic thought as regards natural resources, exposing the serious holes — in some cases, the yawning chasms — in the conventional theory. It concludes by suggesting that what is really needed is not incremental modifications of conventional theory but a thorough reconceptualization of economics — reorganizing economics around the fact that natural resources and the physical environment constitute the ultimate foundation upon which all economic activity is constructed.

Part III examines ways we can sustain the integrity of that environmental foundation through preserving our non-renewable resource base and developing the renewable resource base. It shows how the theory of a renewable resource economy can be turned into concrete practice.

After spending nine years immersed in the public policy arena in Washington, D.C., I harbor no illusions that the road to achieving a renewable resource economy will be a short one or an easy one. But it is one worth traveling. Moreover, we really have no choice.

CONTENTS

I
The Realities

1

GENUINE SUPPLY-SIDE ECONOMICS

The challenges facing the United States in the economic sphere are well known, well documented, and taken very seriously. The challenges facing the United States in the natural resource and environmental sphere are well documented, but they are not as well known and they are not being taken as seriously by leaders in government, business, and labor. Natural resource and environmental issues are often dismissed as irrelevant to the "hard" issues of economic growth, inflation, employment, and productivity. This perspective is faulty.

A major challenge for economists and public leaders in the 1980s is to recognize, understand, and act on one basic fact: *Natural resources and the environment constitute the ultimate foundation upon which all future economic activity must be constructed. From this it follows that future economic progress in the United States will be increasingly dependent on the sustained integrity of the resource and environmental base.* President Theodore Roosevelt perhaps said it best three quarters of a century ago: "It is safe to say that the prosperity of our people depends directly on the energy and intelligence with which our natural resources are used. It is equally clear that these resources are the final basis of national power and perpetuity."[1] To contribute to our understanding of the economy, a genuine supply-side economics must be based on the fact that biological capital (and solar income) is equally as important as financial capital for achieving long-run economic growth. In the economic verbiage about budget cuts, tax cuts, and investment incentives, financiers,

1

economists, politicians, and even business and union leaders have forgotten the source from which all growth, wealth, and economic progress springs — natural resources and the environment.

We live in an era in which our economic prosperity, the condition of our environment, and the quality of our lives will be determined more and more by how carefully we manage our remaining nonrenewable resources and by how successfully we sustain and enhance our renewable resources. We need a judicious blend of investments in rejuvenating our soils, fisheries, forestlands, and recreational resources and changes in our physical resources and energy policies to emphasize conservation to guarantee the wealth and vitality of our resource base as a rich inheritance for future generations. The challenge is great; today's resource and environmental problems are considerably more serious and more complex than ever before.

GLOBAL DIMENSIONS

Much of the new complexity comes from the fact that the interests and actions of other nations must be considered in facing our major resource and environmental problems. A continuing set of interlocking resource shortages is in the offing, which will generate both direct adverse impacts on human well-being and increased international political tensions as the possibility fades that Third and Fourth World nations will ever be able to match the current material prosperity of the wealthy industrial nations. According to one study, to have provided the 1970 world population with the capital stock of industrial materials, per person, that prevailed in 1970 in the ten richest nations would have required, on average, about 60 times the 1970 world production of these materials.[2] It has also been estimated that for the rest of the world to reach a par with the U.S. standard of living, it would have to consume up to 200 times the present production of many of the earth's nonrenewable minerals.[3] While such figures cannot be considered accurate point estimates, it is clear that with present materials-intensive technologies, there is little hope of early prosperity for the poor countries even if global allocation of materials flows were to change dramatically.

The lack of insight in world thinking with respect to these resource problems and the weak political machinery available to deal with them are far from encouraging. Symptomatic of both is the conspicuous lack of preparation for ensuring an adequate supply of key materials in times of emergency. In fact, global inventories for many major commodities are below earlier levels, making the United States and the rest of the world extremely vulnerable to disturbances in materials markets. And yet, talks in the late 1970s aimed at an international wheat agreement ended in failure, and no attempt was made to establish international buffer stocks for feed grains. It remains likely that periodic materials shortages will involve scrambles for supplies and outbursts of speculation of major proportions.

Resort to military action is possible not just in the case of poor countries unwilling to suffer quietly but, with equal or greater likelihood, in the case of industrial powers whose high standard of living is threatened by cutoffs of external resources. Conflicts over access to resources of undefined ownership, such as seabed minerals, constitute a potential tinderbox of growing magnitude.

Just before his death, historian Arnold Toynbee assessed the likely course of the United States and other industrial nations. He foresaw a permanent state of siege for the developed nations as critical resource shortages and mounting pollution forced a wartime austerity on these once-affluent lands. He warned that in the

> developed countries there will be a bitter struggle for the control of their diminished resources. This struggle will merely worsen a bad situation; it will somehow have to be stopped. If left unchecked, it would lead to anarchy and to a drastic reduction of the size of the population by civil war, famine and pestilence, the historic reducers of populations that have outgrown their means of subsistence. Consequently in all developed countries, a new way of life — a severely regimented way — will have to be imposed by a ruthless authoritarian government.[4]

Glimmerings can be seen of an alternative vision — based on acceptance of the physical interconnectedness of the planet. Barbara Ward has written more optimistically of a choice we can make:

> We are thus, in the most fundamental sense, at a hinge of history. If we can learn from the growing evidence of destructive risk in our present practices to determine that the next phase of development shall respect and sustain and even enhance the environment, we can look to a human future. If on the contrary we have learned so little that every present trend toward pollution, disruption, decay, and collapse is merely to be enhanced by its spread all around the planet, then the planet's capacity to sustain such insults will be ineluctably exceeded.[5]

The remainder of this book addresses this fundamental choice, but it does so in a geographically more proscribed and a conceptually more expanded framework. The focus will primarily be limited to the United States because a significant share of any solutions to global problems will come from that nation and because the environmental path of economic development that it follows will have global impact owing to the large proportion of world resources it commands. The focus will be expanded to take "sustaining and enhancing the environment" not as a goal solely for its own sake but as the necessary means for healthy economic growth to continue.

RESOURCES AND ECONOMIC PROGRESS

U.S. historical experience demonstrates the inextricable interrelationship of resources and economic progress most clearly in the interaction of resources with what has been the primary source of economic growth: technology. Much of the unique direction of U.S. technological innovation was due to the intensive exploitation of natural resources that existed in considerable abundance relative to capital and labor.

Drawing on the extensive forests, U.S. technology from the earliest times had been particularly devoted to innovations that promoted wood usage or that reduced the cost of complementary inputs. The abundance of wood also acted as a conservative force in that it caused the United States to lag a full half century behind the more advanced mineral-using technology of the Industrial Revolution.

The main features of the transformation in U.S. agriculture in the nineteenth century bear the distinctive imprint of resource abundance. The very high land-to-labor ratio led to the mechanization of agricultural operations; this, in turn, led to an increase in the acreage that could be cultivated by a single farmer.

Resource abundance similarly affected development in the manufacturing sector, resulting in U.S. leadership in the mass production of standardized products consisting of interchangeable component parts. The United States was able to adopt a machine-using technology very early because its resource abundance provided the opportunity for trading off natural resource inputs for other scarce factors of production.

These factors very quickly thrust the U.S. economy toward the capital- and resource-intensive end of the spectrum of techniques. Certainly if fossil fuels had not been in abundant supply and cheaply available, different technologies, and even a different type of science would likely have developed and led to a very different type of society.

Overall, the early U.S. experience with nature was basically one in which nature was an enemy to be turned into a servant. This resulted in the accumulation of a great deal of practical knowledge about how to use nature but not of much interest in nature for its own sake. The attitude is well captured in Alexis de Tocqueville's description of the pioneer, in contrast with the European, attitude toward nature:

> In Europe people talk a great deal of the wilds of America, but the Americans themselves never think about them: they are insensible to the wonders of inanimate Nature, and they may be said not to perceive the mighty forests which surround them until they fall beneath the hatchet. Their eyes are fixed upon another sight: the . . . march across the wilds — drying swamps, turning the course of rivers, peopling solitudes, and subduing Nature.[6]

To be fair, there were gentler conceptions of nature, particularly in the pastoral or agrarian ideal, which was most eloquently articulated by Thomas Jefferson. According to this perspective, nature and man should be in harmony, a harmony most realized in the husbandry of agriculture, which has no need of cities for its support. Rather than the ideal of subjection, which seems to characterize Bacon and the Puritans, nature had become a possible source of strength: "Those who labour in the earth are the chosen people of God," wrote Jefferson.

Moving to the present, we find that natural resources still play a major and vital role in our society even though we are the world's most highly industrialized nation. Indeed, one of the most consistently strong sectors of our economy is the agricultural sector, which generated $167 billion of farm income in 1981. The critical importance of fuel minerals is well known, but nonfuel minerals also play a major role. The value of processed materials of mineral origin was $240 billion in 1980.

The interrelationship of resources and economic activity can also be demonstrated by examining specific impacts on productivity and inflation. Since the mid-1960s, productivity growth has decelerated in agriculture and become negative in mining. These two trends, reflecting some decline in the average quality of natural resources, led to an average annual 0.2 percentage point reduction in productivity during the 1973–79 period relative to the 1948–66 period. Regarding inflation, there is disagreement among the experts concerning the precise contribution of energy price increases, but there is agreement that they had a significant impact in the 1970s, with estimates ranging as high as a one-third contribution. What is beyond dispute is that in 1972, 1973, and 1974 the world economy experienced an unprecedented increase in primary commodity prices. Within the three-year period, the prices of raw materials rose by 150 percent in world markets and touched off the worst inflation of the post World War II period in the industrial nations.

Throughout the 1970s the relationship between economic growth and environmental protection was often viewed as a trade-off by the proponents of each. In the 1980s we must rid ourselves of this mentality. This is not to say that economic activity has not harmed the environment or that environmental regulations have not adversely affected economic development. Certainly there have been adverse impacts in both directions. The distortion of the truth lies in the exclusive focus on such effects, neglecting the important nuances of each effect and the way in which economic and environmental principles and policies are, or can be made to be, compatible. Environmental protection principles, on one hand, can be used both to preserve the country's natural resource base and to invest wisely in built-up as well as growing metropolitan areas. Eliminating pollution helps revitalize the nation's urban areas and reduce disparities among regions. Economic growth, on the other hand, can be a principal means to achieving quality-of-life objectives, including environmental quality.

Beginning in the 1970s, the perception of limits on our ability to exploit our habitat without regard for the consequences began to lead to fundamental changes in thought and action. We have come to see waste and excess not as the admirable surplus of a productive economy but as simple stupidity — a symptom of social corpulence. The perception of limits, still denied by some, has evoked from others a fresh wave of invention and ingenuity; we see it in the drive toward conservation, in the effort to develop solar energy, and in the reexamination of industrial processes to minimize pollution beforehand rather than having to clean it up afterward. We are finding that the recognition of scarcity can in and of itself be a resource — an intellectual resource that points our technology in a new direction, toward an infinitely more creative mode of invention that keeps human demands in balance with earth's supply.

SUSTAINABLE GROWTH

The concept of sustainable growth encompasses the necessity of continued economic growth to meet basic human needs around the globe while also underscoring that the growth must be of such a nature that it can be sustained indefinitely by respecting nature's boundary conditions.

There is at present no systematic means of quantifying rates of sustainable growth over the long term. What is sustainable in terms of resource limitations or environmental capacity depends on the composition of the basket of goods and services, and that composition keeps changing in response to changing consumption preferences, perceived resource or environmental constraints, and technological capacities. Defining *sustainable* may involve issues of intergenerational equity. Insofar as constraints on growth are institutional and attitudinal, limits raise fundamental questions concerning the differing valuations placed on economic growth by different cultures or by individuals and groups within a given culture.

Nevertheless, despite considerable indeterminancy, some features of what is sustainable are clear. It is easy to point to examples of unsustainably high rates of growth in specific environments — when renewable resources are used beyond their rates of potential regeneration. Destruction of forests, "mining the soil," and polluting rivers and lakes beyond redemption all come to mind. Thus, at a minimum the term *sustainable growth* implies compatibility with limitations of natural resources and environmental absorption capacities.

One thumbnail sketch of how a sustainable world might look will help in visualizing the nature of the possibilities:

> Material well-being would almost certainly be indexed by the quality of the existing inventory of goods, rather than by the rate of physical turnover. Planned obsolescence would be eliminated. Excessive consumption and waste would become causes for embarassment, rather than symbols of prestige.

The environment would be enhanced, and global population would be balanced with the planet's carrying capacity. . . . The inflationary impact of raw materials prices would be diminished, as resource scarcity was mitigated by the widespread use of durable products that could be recycled. Industries and energy sources would be decentralized and hence less vulnerable to acts of man and nature. Both ends of the material chain — the mine and the dump — fade in importance compared with the improvement of the human condition from existing material stocks. Society would, at long last, apply its collective intellect and energy to the central task of an intelligent materials policy: making the most of what we already have.[7]

How do we get from here to there? We begin in the 1980s by moving toward an economic growth pattern that is in accordance with sound environmental and physical principles so as to ensure that the growth is both sustainable and conducive to the quality of life desired by the American people, including (1) a better natural environment, (2) clean, flexible energy sources at reasonable prices, and (3) more livable urban environments.

Movement in this direction would require substantial change in the policies and activities of corporations, consumers, and government. In general there would occur a reversal of the current emphasis on quantity over quality, means over ends, structures over values, and the individual over the commons. Economic cost accounting would be based not solely upon market forces but upon realistic estimates of the long-range future. Recognition of the organic wholeness of life and our basic unity with nature would foster subordination of economic life to profounder human ends.

John Maynard Keynes, who was a solid blend of the great economic theoretician and the practical man of the world, did not think such a world only a fanciful dream. In discussing his hope for the world of his grandchildren, he said:

I see us free, therefore, to return to some of the most secure and certain principles of religion and traditional virture — that avarice is a vice, that the exaction of usury is a misdemeanor, and the love of money is detestable, that those walk most truly in the paths of virtue and sane wisdom who take least thought for the morrow. We shall once more value ends above means and prefer the good to the useful. We shall honor those who can teach us how to pluck the hour and the day virtuously and well, the delightful people who are capable of taking direct enjoyment in things, the lilies of the field who toil not, neither do they spin.[8]

2

U.S. RESOURCE DEPLETION

Important changes in U.S. land use patterns in this century have lately begun to be perceived as land use problems. For food our urban population now largely depends on the vast consolidated farms of the Midwest and arid West rather than on the small farms adjacent to towns and cities, which once provided visual relief and diverse wildlife habitat as well as fresh produce. The changes in the nation's landscape since 1900 can be measured as well by the loss of topsoil, wetlands, and hardwood forests in rural America and by the scarcity of open space easily available for routine urban recreation.

An awareness has grown that positive steps must be taken to protect soils, safeguard critical systems and hazardous geological areas, preserve ecological and cultural diversity, and conserve the amenities of the nation's landscape. It has become increasingly clear that none of our remaining resources can be taken for granted in the face of new and rapid rural growth; continued urban sprawl; demands for new energy, transportation, and industrial development; and other significant changes.

A look at current trends affecting our land, water, and air shows that the physical realities are often harsh, that the problems in each area often feed on each other, and that immediate action on a broad number of fronts is necessary. The challenge is indeed formidable.

AGRICULTURAL LAND

Much of the health of the domestic economy rests on the productivity of the nation's vast agricultural system. In 1981 the value of U.S. agricultural crops totaled about $167 billion, of which about $43 billion was exported. Moreover, total agricultural production has continued to increase over the years. This trend has been evident in all major crops but most notably in corn and soybeans, which rose 60 and 61 percent, respectively, from 1970 to 1980. Most of the increased production has gone for export.

Despite its critical role in the economic health of the nation, we are allowing this vital resource base to both diminish and deteriorate. We are simultaneously losing a significant amount of prime farmland and cropland each year and suffering a steady decline in agricultural productivity. The loss of agricultural land, both quantitatively and qualitatively, will likely be one of the major resource problems of the next two decades. It is also likely to be one of the foremost national challenges the United States will face, for it has wide-ranging economic, social, and political implications.

The trend is clear and well documented. From 1966 to 1977 the United States converted agricultural land to nonagricultural uses (homes, roads, artificial lakes, and so on) at the rate of about 2 to 3 million acres per year[1] — of which about 675,000 acres were from the cropland base[2] and 1 million acres were prime farmland. Although the amount of prime farmland being lost is a small percentage of total U.S. agricultural land (less than 0.1 percent annually), there are two disturbing factors in this trend: first, the land base is fixed; second, conversion to urban uses is essentially irreversible.

Moreover, the real loss in prime agricultural land may be much greater than that indicated by the data showing the amount of land actually converted. In addition to soil erosion, other physical factors have contributed to reductions in the ability of land to grow crops — for example, excessive compaction of the soil from large farming machinery, the accumulation of crop-killing salts in topsoil because of inadequate irrigation practices, and the depletion of available water supplies. Taking into account all of these factors, it is estimated that 4.5 million acres a year were lost permanently from the cropland resource pool between 1967 and 1977. If such rates continued unabated, our total cropland resource base would lose 103 million acres between 1977 and 2000 — land that represents 19 percent of our current crop-growing capability.[3]

The rate of loss has not been uniform and the effect on particular states could be devastating. New England has lost half its native farmland, the Mid-Atlantic states have lost 22 percent of theirs, and the Midwest has lost 9 percent of its cropland. In addition, if present rates of conversion go unchecked, by the year 2000 New Mexico will have lost 44 percent of its prime farmland and Florida will have lost all of its prime farmland. In the arid West, 225 million acres (an area roughly the size of the 13 original states) have undergone severe desertification since Europeans came to the West.

To put the above figures in perspective, the United States has approximately 413 million acres of cropland and about 127 million acres of potential cropland for a total of about 540 million acres. This is only about 23 percent of the country's 2.3 billion acres.

The **1977 National Resource Inventory**[4] also showed that there are 346 million acres defined as "prime farmland." Two thirds of this prime farmland is being used for crops, and one fifth is committed to nonagricultural uses, thus outside the cropland base, leaving about 52 million acres of prime farmland potentially available for future use in crop production. This is only about 10 percent of our total cropland base — not a wide margin for meeting future needs from our most productive segment of farmland.

The extent of these future needs must now be assessed because the question of how critical the supply situation is depends on the projected demand for U.S. agricultural products. The demand side has been divided into three basic components in two recent studies. Since both the categories and the time frame are different in each study, it is instructive to review the conclusions of each.

The **National Agricultural Lands Study** (NALS) conducted by the U.S. Department of Agriculture (USDA) and the Council on Environmental Quality looked at exports, conventional domestic uses, and ethanol (ethyl alcohol distilled from corn) production. Exports are expected to dominate the growth in overall agricultural demand. Over the last two decades of this century, the USDA projects that the volume of U.S. exports will grow by 140 to 250 percent above the 1980 level, assuming constant real commodity prices. Domestic demand for food and fiber is projected to increase about 1 percent annually by volume during the 1980s and then slow to 0.9 percent annually during the 1990s. As real energy prices continue to rise, the use of domestically produced alcohol fuels from crops will increase. The ethanol industry is projected to reach an annual production capacity of from 4 to 6 billion gallons by 1990. The feedstock for this projected production level would require the corn grown on 15 to 23 million acres.

In sum, the volume of demand for U.S. agricultural products is projected to increase by 60 to 85 percent over the 1980 level, assuming constant real prices, by the year 2000. If these demands materialize and if the yield per acre growth rate of the 1970s continues, U.S. farmers will have to cultivate an additional 140 million acres of land for production of principal crops, an increase of about 50 percent. The NALS concludes that though technically possible, shifts of land into cultivation of this magnitude will require some major adjustments in the U.S. agricultural system.

The other set of assessments was undertaken in implementing the Soil and Water Resources Conservation Act of 1977.[5] It was projected that the United States will need to produce 462 million acres of crops by the year 2030 to meet domestic consumption and foreign trade requirements for food and fiber. In addition, if the United States is to produce energy from biomass equal to 10 percent of our liquid fuel requirements, about 127 million additional acres of cropland will have to be put into production. Finally, producing one third to one half of our demand for certain agriculturally produced strategic and essential industrial materials — such as rubber, sperm oil, and castor oil — would require an estimated 60 million additional acres of cropland. The total of these three demand components comes to 649 million acres. Given an estimated 50 million acres of today's cropland that will be converted to other uses by the year 2030, this means that the United States could find itself about 159 million acres short of the cropland needed by that time.

There are more than 540 million acres of land that could be used for crop production if the United States is willing to incur the loss of other products as well as substantially greater economic and natural resource degradation costs for production and much higher prices for food and fiber. To gain additional acreage, the United States would have to eliminate hardwood forests, drain large areas of wetlands, and live with exceedingly high levels of soil erosion on fragile lands.

Specifically, the Soil Conservation Service has estimated that 112 million acres not currently in production could be used for agriculture, but such conversion would be at the expense of 82 million acres of pasture and 24 million acres of forests, which together include 23 million acres of wetlands. Thus the costs are high: decreased timber production, decreased seafood production and marine life in the long run, decreased wildlife habitats, increased stream siltation and surface water pollution, degradation of the underground water supply, and, eventually, decreased productivity of our agricultural land base.

The decline in agricultural productivity has already begun. This is an extremely serious trend because unless it is reversed, the adverse economic consequences from the quantitative loss of agricultural land will be magnified by qualitative losses as well. The decline has been dramatic. From a 1960s average annual growth rate of 1.6 percent, the yield per acre dropped by more than half to 0.7 percent in the 1970s. This meant that in the 1970s about three quarters of the gain in agricultural production came from newly cultivated acreage and only one fourth from increased yield per acre.

The NALS identified four main factors that dampened the productivity growth:

- The rising costs of fuel, fertilizers, and other energy-intensive inputs,
- Less fertile agricultural land available for cropland uses,
- Lack of reserve supplies of water to sustain past growth rates in irrigated agriculture, and
- The loss of natural soil fertility due to erosion or salinization.[6]

Since the second factor has been touched on and the third is discussed in a later section, the first and fourth factors will now be touched upon.

Much of the historical increase in yields per acre is the result of massive applications of petroleum-based fertilizers. In 1980, 53 million tons were applied to U.S. cropland, a threefold increase over 1950. Furthermore, twice the amount of synthetic pesticides were used in 1976 as in 1964.[7] The fundamental problem is that subsequent fertilizer applications bring lower and lower increases in yield. For example, each additional million pounds of fertilizer applied to U.S. cornfields brought an average of 770,000 bushels of corn between 1959 and 1964 and only 130,000 additional bushels between 1964 and 1970. The harsh fact is that there is not much U.S. cropland that could benefit substantially from the application of additional fertilizer.

This is likely to lead to more land-extensive production, requiring more acres to maintain gross production levels. Large-scale movements in this direction are already occurring in the adoption of "short season" cotton in the Southwest and minimum tillage practices for a number of commodities across the nation. Cultivation of lower yielding drought-tolerent cereals could become a major movement in the direction of more land-extensive domestic production.

Soil erosion and the resulting sedimentation problems to crop, range, forest, and pasturelands are among the most pervasive problems of resource management. The facts are startling. Since the country's founding, at least a third of the topsoil on U.S. croplands has been lost (the average depth is down from 12 inches to 7 or 8 inches). Some of the richest agricultural lands, such as those in Iowa, have lost about half their topsoil. For each ton of corn produced by an Iowa farmer in 1977, five tons of soil eroded from that state's land. Nationally, over 6.4 billion tons of soil a year are lost in water and wind erosion — the highest level in the nation's history; 83 percent of this (5.3 billion tons) is from agricultural land, and more than half (equivalent to 89 tons per second) is from cropland. All of this — despite the estimated $15 to $30 billion devoted to controlling soil erosion over the past 40 years.

Soil erosion is far from uniform. The national average of 4.8 tons per acre in 1977 masks large discrepancies. Almost a third of our agricultural land is experiencing very little erosion (less than one ton per acre per year), accounting for just over 2 percent of total erosion. At the other extreme, slightly less than 3 percent of our land (including some of our best cropland) is eroding at a rate of more than 25 tons per acre per year, which amounts to almost a third of total erosion.[8] Six counties actually suffered losses of over 100 tons per acre. Of particular concern is the fact that over half the cropland erosion occurs in the Corn Belt and the Northern Plains since the Corn Belt is one of the most productive agricultural areas in the world.

Erosion nearly always reduces soil productivity. One serious effect is the annual loss of more than 50 million tons of plant nutrients (nitrogen, phosphorus, and potassium) from U.S. cropland. To replace all of the nitrogen and phosphorus and one fourth of the potassium lost by soil erosion just in 1979 would have cost $18 billion.

A different perspective on how productivity is affected can be gained by examining the impact on corn yields. In the southern Piedmont, a six-inch reduction in topsoil has reduced average corn yields by 41 percent. In western Tennessee similar soil erosion reduced corn yields 42 percent. A general rule of thumb is that the loss of 1 inch of topsoil from a base of 12 inches (150 tons on one acre) generally reduces corn yields between two and three bushels on that acre. Based on this reduction in yield and assuming corn prices of $3 per bushel, the USDA has estimated that topsoil is worth 54¢ to 81¢ per ton based solely on the soil's contribution to crop production.[9]

The effect of soil erosion on national productivity has also been estimated by examining the loss in terms of acre-equivalents.[10] These acre-equivalents are not discrete acres being washed away in one dramatic event; they represent the slow, imperceptible loss being cumulatively suffered over millions of acres of U.S. farmland. On this basis, cropland is losing — to sheet and rill erosion alone — about 1.01 million acre-equivalents annually. Wind erosion in the ten Great Plains states would add 0.24 million acre-equivalents. This suggests that over the next 50 years the loss of productivity due to erosion of croplands will be equivalent to the loss of 62.5 million acres.

The principal conclusion to be drawn, regardless of the precise accuracy of the estimates, is that the current rate of productivity loss, however one chooses to convert it to numerical values, is far too high. It can, and should be, drastically lowered.

Table 2.1 provides an interesting way to summarize many of the trends described above and their implications for agricultural output in the year 2000.[11] The outlook is quite disturbing. If current trends in productivity increases continue, production will be 139 million tons short of what is needed if the United States is to meet projected demand, both domestic and export. Even if an optimistic 1.1 percent annual productivity increase were achieved, we would still be 83 million tons short. In terms of exports, continuation of current trends would mean only 30 million tons available for export in 2000 (about one fifth of 1978 exports), and a 1.1. percent productivity increase would mean 86 million tons for export, less than two thirds of 1978 exports and half the amount the USDA projects will be needed for export in 2000. Clearly, the U.S. farming industry, American consumers, and the global community so dependent on U.S.

TABLE 2.1

Effect on U.S. Corn, Wheat, Soybean, Sorghum, and Hay Production in 2000 of Cropland Conversion, Soil Erosion, Groundwater Decline, and Productivity Gains

	Millions of Tons
In 1978, production of these five crops was	472
If all our potential cropland were planted today, production would rise to	616
But if current trends in cropland loss continue to 2000, production would fall to	499
And if energy and industrial crops are planted on 18 million acres of our cropland, production would fall to	478
And if the acres with soil erosion of more than five tons per acre per year lose 10 percent of their productivity, production would fall to	470
And if the acres now irrigated with groundwater that is being severly overdrafted are converted to dryland farming, production would fall to	455
And if technological advances increase yields per acre 1. 1.1 percent every year to 2000, production would rise to	579
2. according to current trends (0.7 percent during the 1980s and 0.5 percent to 2000), production would rise to	523

Source: Courtesy of Mary La Webb and Judith Jacobsen, *U.S. Carrying Capacity: An Introduction* (Washington, D.C.: Carrying Capacity, 1982), p. 32.

agriculture face the prospect of seriously disruptive changes in the next two decades. We are indeed closer to the carrying capacity of our agricultural lands as we use them today than the common perception of the United States as the world's breadbasket would have us believe.

FORESTS

When Europeans first came to the New World, about 950 million acres of what became the United States was covered with trees. Of this, about 90 percent was "commercially productive" by today's standards. Today that forested acreage has shrunk to 740 million acres, and only 65 percent of it is commercially productive. Moreover, the U.S. Forest Service projects that if current trends continue, demand for wood from U.S. forests is likely to surpass supplies by 1990.[12]

Of today's total forestland the federal government owns more than one third, with the rest divided between large corporations and "nonindustrial" private owners. The federal government is required by law to manage its lands to satisfy a number of different uses, including timber production, mining, recreation, wildlife habitat, and so forth. The principal focus of large industrial owners is, of course, on timber production. In many ways the key group is the private, nonindustrial owners, for they hold 58 percent of the commercial forestland.

A recent assessment of the U.S. commercial timber situation, published in 1980, portrayed a rather optimistic picture in terms of activity over the last three decades. It showed that total net timber growth increased 9.6 percent between 1970 and 1976 — an average rate of 1.6 percent a year. In 1976 the net growth of softwood timber rose 9.3 percent and exceeded removals by roughly 22 percent, while hardwood timber net growth rose 10 percent, exceeding removals by 124 percent.[13] This is substantial improvement over 1952 conditions when growth and removals of softwoods were about equal, while growth of hardwoods was about 52 percent greater than removals. Though this appears to convey a solid situation regarding U.S. forests, it masks a number of potentially very troublesome problems.

First, national statistics hide important variations among regions and among types of timber. For example, in the Pacific Coast region, annual harvests have exceeded annual growth since at least 1952. The problem is particularly severe for softwood sawtimber, which is timber suitable for lumber. The situation in Oregon also illustrates the seriousness of the problem of overcutting privately held forestland, particularly land held by large companies. In Oregon the big timber growers are cutting at a rate that will nearly exhaust their softwood inventories by the middle of the next decade. These inventories totaled 119.5 billion board feet in 1952, but by 1977 they had shrunk to 59 billion and by 1990 they could plummet to 5 billion.

A second problem is the loss of timberland to development, cropland, pastureland, and other uses, which is likely to reduce future timber supplies. Between 1962 and 1977 about 2 million acres of commercial forestland were lost on average every year, leaving a total of 438 million acres. Further losses of timberland can be expected.

The USDA projects that the forestland area will decrease by 3 percent annually by the year 2030 (about 0.4 million acres per year or a total of 20 million acres). In the 1980s a significant portion of the decline will result from conversion to cropland, particularly in the Southeast. The USDA further projects that in the 1990s most of the conversion will be to reservoirs, urban areas, highways and airport construction, and surface-mining sites. However, about 32 million acres of potential cropland are now classified as forestland. Consequently, if a strong demand develops for cropland, the decrease in forest area will be somewhat larger than the USDA's projection.

A third problem revolves around the fact that more than half the economically productive forest acreage is owned by 4 million people, mainly farmers. Any significant expansion in U.S. wood production must be based on more wood being grown on and taken from these usually small, scattered woodlots. But private owners usually hold their forests for purposes other than wood production — for recreation, grazing, or aesthetic reasons. Furthermore, most owners are not interested in making the investments required to increase harvests from their lots because decades must elapse before such practices as reseeding and intensive management yield a financial return.

Finally, we face a serious productivity problem in that the average annual growth of commercial forests is only about 61 percent of potential growth. In particular, it is the low average productivity in the Pacific Coast region that is of the greatest concern. Current growth in that region's national forests is only a third of its potential, and that on forest industry lands is two thirds of its potential. Another factor reducing forest productivity — particularly in the northeastern United States — is acid rain (discussed in Chapter 3).

The management of forests falls under the Forest and Rangeland Resources Planning Act of 1974 (RPA). This act requires the Department of Agriculture to assess and inventory the nation's forest- and rangelands every ten years and the secretary of agriculture to recommend to the president every five years a Renewable Resources Program for "management and administration of the National Forest System, for research, and for cooperative state and private Forest Service Programs." The program, completed in 1980, was designed to achieve a balance among three important factors: economic efficiency, environmental quality, and the social values related to Forest Service activities.

WATER

The nation's water situation is analogous to that of forests: we have an abundance of water, but we also have an abundance of problems. Moving from the East to the West illustrates the wide variety of water problems the country is facing.[14] In the East around 1980, the major old cities such as New York, Boston, and Philadelphia were all losing 10 to 50 percent of their fresh water from leaky mains. Some farmers in the Midwest use the wasteful irrigation technique of flooding the land because they get federal surface water for only about $1 an acre foot, while other farmers not lucky enough to be near a federal water project are struggling to make ends meet by pumping well water from beneath their land at an annual cost of $50 to $75 an acre for fuel. In the arid West, whole river systems have dried up, others are choked with sediment washed from denuded land, and hundreds of thousands of acres of previously irrigated cropland have been abandoned to wind or weeds — all this despite the fact that around 1980 western states consumed more than 12 times more water per capita than the eastern states. In total about 225 million acres of land are undergoing severe desertification, an area roughly the size of the 13 original states. In California, where there are enormous legal obstacles involved in the transfer of surface water rights, farmers with plentiful water grow low-value cash crops like alfalfa on poor land, while that water remains unavailable to others with better land who could sow high-return crops like melons.

The Second National Water Assessment highlighted a number of critical water resource problems in need of attention by all levels of government:

- Inadequate surface water supply. Although local water supply problems occur in all parts of the nation, several local areas in the Midwest and far West have now or will have serious surface water problems by the year 2000.
- Overdraft of groundwater. Serious groundwater overdrafts, resulting in declining water tables, are occurring in the High Plains area and in parts of Arizona.
- Pollution of surface and groundwater. Surface and groundwater pollution occur in most areas of the country. Maintenance of both surface and groundwater quality for drinking is of concern nationwide but especially in rural areas where drinking water receives little or no treatment.
- Flooding. In 1975 alone, 107 persons were killed by floodwaters, and property damage was estimated at $3.4 billion. Such damage will increase to $4.3 billion annually by the year 2000 unless there is increased floodplain management and control of unwise floodplain development.[15]

Although the United States has ample surface and underground water resources, the uneven distribution of these resources has produced some serious local and regional water shortages. Arizona claims that its supply of water already falls short of its needs by 2.3 million acre-feet a year (an *acre-foot of water*, 326,000 gallons, is enough to cover an acre to a depth of one foot). California is said to have a current shortage of 3 million acre-feet and West Texas 4 million. Though generally associated with the arid West, such shortages have occurred at various times in other parts of the nation as well.

Water shortages generally reflect inadequate surface and groundwater sources, especially where water is intensively used to satisfy multiple demands such as irrigated agriculture, municipal and industrial supplies, energy production, recreation, and maintenance of fish and wildlife habitats. But shortages of usable water can also be caused by poor water quality.

Groundwater—defined as subsurface water that occurs beneath a water table in soils or rocks or in geologic formations that are fully saturated—is a vast natural resource; its volume is estimated at about 50 times the annual flow of surface water. The Water Resources Council estimates that 33 to 59 quadrillion gallons of fresh groundwater occur within one-half mile of the surface, enough to supply withdrawals at current rates for 200 to 300 years.[16]

Groundwater supplies 25 percent of the fresh water used for all purposes in the country. About half the population depends on groundwater for its domestic water supply. Approximately 30 trillion gallons of fresh groundwater were withdrawn for all uses in 1975: for irrigation, 69 percent; industry, 14 percent; urban drinking water, 13 percent; and rural drinking water, 5 percent. In the 25 years from 1950 to 1975, the use of fresh groundwater increased over 140 percent.

Many parts of the country are using groundwater at rates exceeding natural recharge (that is, the water is being mined). In 1975 approximately 25 percent of all groundwater withdrawals were overdrafts, mostly in agricultural regions of the arid West. In 1980, 21 billion more gallons each day flowed out than seeped in. This practice has many undesirable effects. It causes problems with diminishing artesian pressure, declining spring and stream flow, land subsidence, and saltwater intrusion. As long as the water remaining in storage underground is still relatively plentiful and accessible, mining the water is likely to continue. Yet these continued withdrawals without compensating recharge merely defer the inevitable day when alternative sources must be found or serious decisions must be made concerning the continued existence of water-dependent industries, irrigated agriculture, or residential communities. In the meantime, irreversible environmental damage may have occurred; for example, subsurface compaction and land subsidence may damage the aquifer to the extent that it will never fully recharge.

Overdrafting occurs in both urban and rural areas. Tucson, the largest U.S. city to depend entirely on groundwater, in 1981 pumped water out of the ground at five times the rate nature puts it back in. By 1981 it had purchased and retired from use about 12,000 acres of farmland to augment its water supply by gaining control of irrigation water rights. City officials anticipate the need to purchase another 36,000 acres of land by 1985 and have budgeted about $120 million for that purpose. This figure pales in comparison with the other "solution." Currently under construction, the Central Arizona Project will divert 1.2 million acre-feet of water per year from the Colorado River. The official estimate of the cost is $1.5 billion, but another study estimates that the project will cost U.S. taxpayers $5.4 billion over the next 50 years.

The pattern is a familiar one in the arid West. A local economy is built and thrives on the depletion of groundwater. Then, when it becomes apparent the resource will not last, an expensive water-import project is launched.

Urbanization elsewhere in the arid West is causing similar abandonment of cropland. Some 50,000 acres of formerly irrigated cropland have been abandoned to serve the water needs of the growing Pueblo and Colorado Springs metropolitan area. Dryland farming is not practical, and conversion to perennial grassland requires time and money.

Overdraft of groundwater is just as serious a problem for agriculture areas as it is for urban settlements. The prime example is the problem of the Ogallala aquifer. Six High Plains states are dependent on the Ogallala: Texas, New Mexico, Oklahoma, Colorado, Kansas, and Nebraska. The situation varies from place to place according to the thickness of the aquifer and the local history of water use. In some parts the water table has dropped 100 feet since 1950 when irrigation began. Engineering studies indicate that underground water in the region may be depleted in 3 to 20 years. The High Plains of West Texas and eastern New Mexico alone contain the largest irrigable landmass in the world: 52 million acres, roughly equal in size to Kansas (the fourteenth largest state). Nearly 10 million acres presently irrigated in this region are threatened by continued removal of groundwater in excess of recharge rates. Much of our domestically produced cotton is grown on this land.

What lies ahead for West Kansas is a transition from irrigated corn agriculture to the production of less water-intensive crops and, perhaps ultimately, to dryland farming of wheat and grain sorghums. In extreme cases in Texas, exhaustion of the aquifer has resulted in the land's return to sagebrush.

The case of Gaines County in Texas is illustrative of the problem at large. The entire billion-dollar-plus agricultural economy of the Texas High Plains is built upon the overdraft of water from the Ogallala. Yet if this overdraft continues, as it is expected to, it will (according to the Texas Department of Water Resources) ultimately result in reduced well yields, reduced acreage irrigated, and reduced agricultural production. Given such concerns, Texas's continued nonregulation of water is difficult to understand. The only method used to regulate the amount of groundwater pumped on the Texas High Plains is well spacing, which means that Texas law continues to regard most groundwater as a mysterious blessing legitimately subject to capture and use in unlimited quantities by any property owner who digs or drives a well. As a consequence, there exists a negative incentive to conserve the resource. It is in fact the "tragedy of the commons" all over again.

It is clear that in the absence of an alternative source of water supply or effective water conservation measures, some irrigated lands now dependent on groundwater mining will revert to dryland uses such as grazing. Farm income and production from such lands will decline drastically.

Given such depletion trends, the irony is that so much irrigation water is wasted. A General Accounting Office study concluded that more than 50 percent of all the country's irrigation water is wasted.[17] The reason is that water is kept so cheap by huge federal subsidies that farmers have little incentive to adopt water-saving irrigation systems, which require a relatively large capital investment. As a result the Southwest's farm economy as a whole is producing less food than it might and less wealth. The Rand Corporation estimated that in 1978 California alone was losing between $60 million and $370 million annually from the inefficient use of water.[18]

To summarize the water situation in the arid West, federal expenditures have encouraged patterns of human settlements and resource development that are not environmentally and economically sustainable. It is possible that the High Plains will seek federal help to import surface water from Mississippi when groundwater supplies become uneconomical. Further requests for federal funds may be expected to rescue the expanding metropolitan areas of the arid zone when their existing surface and groundwater supplies approach exhaustion. In an era of tight federal budgets, inflation, and rising energy prices, public debate about the costs and benefits of federal aid and support for potentially unsustainable settlement patterns and use of land will undoubtedly increase.

Finally, there is in addition to the problem of groundwater supply the increasingly serious problem of contamination, particularly in other areas of the country that do not face the West's supply problem. The most important source of groundwater contamination is the disposal of industrial wastes at industrial impoundments and solid waste disposal sites. Other major sources are septic tanks, municipal waste water, mining, and petroleum exploration and production. Toxic material, including chemicals and industrial discharges, is seeping into once-pure aquifers, endangering the drinking water of about half the people in the United States who get their water from wells. Surveys show that water supplies in hundreds of communities are so contaminated that they are not safe to drink. The seriousness of the problem is compounded by the fact that the contamination of groundwater is almost irreversible. Water moves sluggishly underground and purifies itself slowly if at all.

AIR QUALITY

New York City in 1974 and Chicago in 1975 had 270 days and 240 days, respectively, of unhealthful, very unhealthful, or hazardous air.[19] Just a few years later, in 1980, the number of days in the three highest risk categories had dropped to 131 and 48, respectively, declines of 51 percent and 80 percent. Overall, from 1974 to 1980 the average number of days of high-risk air for 23 major metropolitan areas declined by 39 percent, from 97 to 59. Thus progress in controlling air pollution has been significant, at least with respect to the more common pollutants.

This is not to say that the problem is solved. Far from it. Many areas still experience pollution levels above the standards established to protect human health, and some cities have actually become much worse. Houston saw its number of days in the three highest categories increase from 35 to 101 between 1974 and 1980. And even though Los Angeles's air quality improved, it still had 221 days in the three highest categories in 1980 (compared with nearly 300 in 1974).

The amount of progress achieved varies considerably from one type of pollutant to another. Particulates — which are solid particles or liquid droplets small enough to remain suspended in air — have perhaps shown the most dramatic improvement. They can irritate the human respiratory system and contribute to acute respiratory illness. The principal sources of man-made particulate emissions are stationary industrial sources (66 percent), vehicles (18 percent), and solid waste disposal (5 percent). Ambient levels of particulates were 31 percent lower in 1980 than they were in 1960. Three fourths of this change occurred before the Environmental Protection Agency (EPA) was established in 1971 as a result of conversions from coal to cleaner fuels and of state and local government requirements for emissions reductions. Estimated particulate emissions decreased by 56 percent between 1970 and 1980, a decline attributable to pollution controls placed on coal-burning facilities and industrial processes and to decreases in the burning of coal and solid waste.

Sulfur dioxide (SO_2) is associated with increases in acute and chronic respiratory diseases and can cause increased death rates, particularly among people with heart and lung diseases, when high concentrations of it are found with high concentrations of particulates. SO_2 emissions result principally (80 percent) from combustion of fossil fuels, mostly by electric utilities. Again, considerable progress has been made in reducing SO_2 pollution. Ambient levels decreased 58 percent between 1966 and 1971, primarily from the use of cleaner fuels in most urban areas. Ambient SO_2 levels continued to decrease in the 1970s, dropping 24 percent between 1974 and 1980.

Ozone, a principal component of smog, is one of the most pervasive pollutants. It impairs breathing and severely irritates mucous membranes of the nose and throat. It is the product of petrochemical reactions between nitrogen oxides and volatile organic compounds (VOCs). Principal sources of VOCs are industrial processes (nearly 50 percent) and vehicles (just over 33 percent). Ambient levels of ozone declined nearly 10 percent between 1974 and 1979.

Carbon monoxide (CO) from motor vehicles interferes with the absorption of oxygen by red blood cells, thereby slowing reflexes, causing drowsiness, and weakening judgment. Ambient levels decreased by 41 percent between 1970 and 1980. Still, in 1980 CO levels found in 145 counties or parts of counties exceeded the health-based ambient standard, 35 percent of these by more than 100 percent.

Finally, the trend in nitrogen dioxide (NO_2) levels stands in sharp contrast to the four pollutants just discussed as ambient levels have increased. NO_2 can irritate the lungs, contribute to respiratory difficulty, and lower resistance to respiratory infections. Emissions come about equally from vehicles and power plants. Between 1974 and 1980 ambient NO_2 levels increased by a total of 5.7 percent.

Two other air pollution problems, both of which may be aggravated by efforts to achieve energy self-sufficiency, are of increasing concern: acid rain and the quality of air indoors. Since acid rain is a global atmospheric problem, it is discussed in Chapter 3.

The presence of air pollutants in homes, including nitrogen oxides and other toxic substances, is just beginning to be analyzed and assessed. There are several reasons for being concerned about indoor air quality. First, most people are indoors most of the time. Even moderate concentrations of pollutants encountered indoors, then, are potentially significant. Second, as homeowners, landlords, and commercial and industrial establishments insulate their dwellings and buildings in response to rising energy prices, they may seal in not only warm or cool air but stale and possibly polluted air as well. Prior to major energy conservation efforts, the average home experienced approximately one air change per hour. But vigorous private conservation efforts may reduce home ventilation to an average of 0.2 to 0.3 air changes per hour. In that event, indoor air pollution may well become more serious.

Indoor pollutants that are of concern include several that are regulated outdoors under the National Ambient Air Quality Standards and other air regulations. CO and NO_2 are emitted from gas stoves and unvented space heaters, sometimes resulting in indoor pollution concentrations that exceed national ambient (outdoor) standards. Two other pollutants that may adversely affect indoor air quality are formaldehyde (a common ingredient in plywood and particle board, foam insulation, furniture, carpets, drapes, and other household items) and radon gas (produced indoors by a wide variety of substances from building materials such as concrete or brick to the soil under building foundations).

MINERALS

Mineral resources constitute the world of nonrenewable resources in contrast to the renewable resources discussed up to this point. Apart from a few large meteorites, there is no mineral income similar to the energy income from the sun, which is instrumental in the renewing of land, forests, water, and air. There are, to be sure, slow processes of concentration taking place in seabed rifts. But these processes take place over eons. We must, for all practical purposes, consider the supply of minerals unchanging — they are an inheritance, not income.

Until recently, minerals have been the "quiet" resource. One did not hear much about them. Yet industrial growth in the United States during this century has been dependent on a wide variety of high-quality mineral resources. In addition to minerals used for energy (coal, oil, gas, and uranium), about 100 other mineral commodities are consumed in agriculture, manufacturing, and other basic industries. Consumption of major nonfuel minerals increased substantially in the first three post–World War II decades. While population increased 49 percent from 1948 to 1978, the consumption of ferrous metals increased 83 percent; phosphate rock, lime, and salt, 235 percent; and aluminum, 650 percent. More then 2 billion tons of nonfuel minerals were consumed in 1977 by the chemical, machinery, electrical, construction, and transportation industries.

The formerly quiet resource has emerged at the heart of a number of major issues or policy areas. Specifically, supply prospects and anticipated prices of raw materials pose a series of foreign and domestic policy issues: stockpiles, trade policy, commodity agreements, investment agreements, governmental organization, recycling, and research and development.

The one issue, however, that has brought minerals into the limelight has been the question of import dependency. Business leaders, in particular, have been sounding an alarm about the nation's heavy dependence on imported strategic minerals. They worry over the fact that imports meet more than 50 percent of our requirements for 20 important minerals.

To ascertain the seriousness of the import threat, the issue of domestic supply potential must be addressed. Here one finds that the question of resource availability for the United States is subject to great dispute. There are two polar views — one that exhaustion is inevitable and the other that humanity through its inventiveness will always be able to counteract any possible effect of scarcity — but most opinions fall in the middle ground. The mild optimists see rising prices acting as a danger signal, discouraging the use of scarce minerals and stimulating technology and the use of alternative materials and energy sources. The mild pessimists, acknowledging that the price mechanism will effectively ration scarce materials, point out that as the fraction of the society's total resources that must be allocated to the resources extraction and production sector grows, there will be fewer resources available for increasing real income.

The answer as to which of these four perspectives will actually be played out over the next two decades will depend a great deal on developments in energy availability and environmental controls. Energy is perhaps the critical factor. With sufficient energy, we will be free to use our technological powers to resolve a great many raw materials problems. Without sufficient energy, resource extraction will encounter numerous difficulties. Copper provides an illustration. It is an important material for industrial society, and it is found in abundance in the earth's crust. But most of it is found in low-grade ores. For example, the grade in one large mine today is only 5.8 pounds of copper per ton of ore. There is no question that we can get copper from the low-grade ores that are so common, but only if we have the energy to operate the large machines that can handle vast amounts of rock — to dig it out of the ground, transport it, crush it, process it into copper, and haul away the spent ore. As long as we have the energy, copper supplies are virtually inexhaustible. But if we do not have the energy, the low-grade resources will be almost as unreachable as they were to primitive man and could be worked only in very small amounts.

Environmental controls will also influence the availability and rate of extraction of mineral resources. The mining and processing of minerals have resulted at certain times and in certain locations in severe adverse effects on the land, on air and water quality, and on human health and safety. Although most mining wastes can be controlled by conventional methods, some operations (uranium phosphate, oil shale, and lead) produce solid, gaseous, and liquid wastes that are difficult to control with existing technology. Major environmental problems include sediment, fugitive dust, release of toxic materials, radioactivity, tailings containment, and organic and inorganic air pollutants.

This environmental constraint is part of a broader societal preference constraint. For example, although the United States possesses enough coal to permit energy self-sufficiency for at least the next century, the scars left by strip mining are heavy environmental costs, and dangers to miners are heavy social costs that currently prevent a rush to increased coal consumption.

The United States is confronted with a serious race between technological progress and the economic depletion of its resource endowment. This is true even when taking into account imports because burgeoning worldwide demand may act as an increasing constraint. To date, technology has been the victor, and many argue that new technologies will arise and so increase efficiency in extracting and using resources that future challenges will be met. Most experts, however, agree that it is a major unknown as to whether the technologies will be able to offset the hard fact that owing to continuing resource depletion given inputs of labor, capital, energy, and other factor inputs will yield less output of energy and resources. Certainly unproductive U.S. efforts to develop commercially available synthetic fuels or oil shale should prompt caution.

What does seem likely to occur during the last two decades of this century is a substantial increase in the real cost of most natural resources, owing both to "imperfections" in market systems and institutional arrangements as well as to the fact that many of the real costs involved in present mineral production and consumption will be paid in the future. Also, U.S. fuel and nonfuel mineral import dependency, already high, will likely be substantially higher in the year 2000.

This question of import dependency deserves closer attention. There are two critical aspects to the import dependency issue: degree of reliance and the countries involved in U.S. reliance. Both are troublesome.

Although there are 20 minerals for which we are more than 50 percent reliant, the concern over import dependency boils down to the four major strategic metals that evidenced high import dependency ratios in 1982: 98 percent for manganese, essential to steel making; 91 percent for cobalt, used in cutting tools as well as jet engines; 85 percent for platinum group metals, catalysts in chemical reactions, telecommunications, and air pollution abatement equipment; and 90 percent for chromium, essential for making stainless steel.[20] These metals (and around 20 more) are termed *strategic* because they are vital to defense and industry but are available in large supplies only from foreign sources.

Of these four, manganese is of the least concern because there is a substantial stockpile, there are low-grade deposits to turn to, and it is abundant in deep-sea nodules, which are ready to be mined as soon as the Law of the Sea Treaty is finalized. Cobalt is of more concern because Zambia and Zaire, both unstable nations, produce two thirds of the world's supply. Fortunately, there is a more-than-two-year supply stockpiled, deep-sea nodules contain cobalt, and even a substantial price increase would not cause a large price increase in the final manufactured product. Finally, platinum and chromium are of greatest concern because if supplies from South Africa become unavailable, the United States would be dependent on its second largest supplier: the Soviet Union. Platinum, used primarily by the auto industry but also in oil refining and other industrial processes, has only a five-month stockpile supply.

Chromium is the mineral with the greatest disruption potential. A National Academy of Sciences study of chromium concluded: "The fact that the United States is strategically more vulnerable to a long-term chromium embargo than to an embargo of any other natural resource, including petroleum, has not been recognized."[21] The Joint Economic Committee did recognize this in the summer of 1980 in reaching a similar conclusion after studying the nation's mineral requirements. Chromium is a workhorse metal used in big tonnages; it is essential for making stainless steel, used in corrosion-resistant tubing and other parts in many key industries. For this reason it has been argued that if there were a chromium embargo, the effects on our basic industries would be felt immediately, resulting in crippling damage to the industrial economy.

What must be remembered is that western Europe and Japan are more dependent than the United States and that global demand for metals is rising steadily. It has been estimated that global consumption will at least double by the turn of the century. A government study warns that by 2000 the U.S. mineral trade deficit will approach $100 billion in current dollars.[22] The message is clear.

Mineral import dependency amounts to a potential strategic threat and thus deserves serious attention and subsequent action.

WASTE

Before leaving the domestic physical realities, the other end of the resource cycle — waste — must be examined. It is an important issue both because the problem has become quite serious and because there is considerable potential for utilizing waste as a significant source of new resources.

The costs of waste pervade all areas of society, and they are considerably higher than most people realize:

- Consumers in the United States spend $4 billion per year just to collect and dispose of wastes (and this figure ignores hidden costs). By 1985 the price will be $6 billion a year.
- Cleaning up the 1200 most dangerous hazardous waste sites in the United States (the cost of avoiding another Love Canal) would cost $22 billion.
- Americans throw away enough organic wastes to produce the energy equivalent of 80 million barrels of oil a year. That's $2.2 billion worth — enough to run the entire country for four days.
- The United States wastes 1% of its energy budget on throwaway beverage containers. Using returnables could cut that figure in half.
- American consumers spend 9% of their grocery bills on packaging they throw out.
- While paper prices skyrocket with recurring shortages and people debate how much more can be harvested from limited forest resources, two-thirds of the annual paper production in the United States ends up in the trash.
- Wastes hurts America's balance of payments. The United States imports 91% of its aluminum, then throws most of it out (over one million tons annually, worth over $400 million to industry).[23]

The two major categories of waste are municipal solid waste and hazardous wastes. Total U.S. municipal waste was estimated at 154 million tons for 1978, the equivalent of 1,440 pounds per person. The amount of municipal waste generated per person also increased over-all for the decade, declining somewhat during 1974 and 1975 but then rising again to an average level of 3.85 pounds per day in 1978. The rate of increase per person for the 1970–78 period averaged approximately 1 percent annually. During this period, labor and equipment costs associated with waste disposal also rose.

As the economics and politics of waste disposal have changed, so has environmental awareness. Solid waste disposal is now coming under much more stringent regulation than in the past. The Resource Conservation and Recovery Act, passed by Congress in 1976, set as an objective the complete elimination of open dumps and the upgrading of other waste disposal practices. It offered federal help to states to create waste management plans and to bring waste disposal systems up to federal standards. These changes could easily double the cost of landfilling wastes in many areas.

We have recently become aware of a whole new generation of environmental problems that can be summarized as the legacy of the chemical age. Showing up as hazardous wastes and as chemicals in our daily lives (400 new ones are introduced each year), they can cause genetic alteration, neurological damage, and fertility loss — the subtle, degenerative kinds of effects that come from long-term exposure to fairly low levels of certain kinds of contaminants.

Indeed, the problem of hazardous waste disposal, epitomized by the Love Canal tragedy, is the most urgent environmental challenge facing U.S. industry today. Of the more than 77 billion pounds of hazardous waste — excluding radioactive materials — generated each year, the EPA reports that a startling 90 percent is disposed of in an unsound fashion. As a result an estimated 800 disposal sites around the nation now pose a potentially significant danger to man and the environment. Just to contain them will cost an estimated $4 billion total and to clean them up completely could take a staggering $44 billion.

3

GLOBAL RESOURCE IMBALANCE

Resource and environmental problems increasingly fail to respect national boundaries. Many of the most serious and complex environmental problems still remaining are inherently global in nature, and hence their solution requires international cooperation on an unprecedented scale.

The next two decades will bring unprecedented strains on the earth's natural systems and resources. The likelihood that each of many complex problem areas could be "resolved" without dangerous side effects seems small. The direction of such global resource–environmental trends is very difficult to change. Few, if any, of the problems are amenable to quick technological or policy fixes; rather, they are inextricably mixed with the world's most perplexing social and economic problems.

The evidence of such a global challenge came in discrete pieces throughout the 1970s, ultimately bringing recognition by the United States government in its **Global 2000 Report**, released in July 1980. This study, the culmination of a three-year effort to discover the long-term implications of present world trends in population, natural resources, and the environment, arrived at a dramatic conclusion:

> If present trends continue, the world in 2000 will be more crowded, more polluted, less stable ecologically, and more vulnerable to disruption than the world we live in now. Serious stresses involving population, resources, and environment are clearly visible ahead.[1]

While the potential for running out of economically accessible nonrenewable resources—the focus of most studies to date—is serious, it is far overshadowed by the potential destruction of renewable resources systems' capacity to reproduce. Unquestionably, the rapidly growing world population is straining the earth's carrying capacity today. A forested area the size of Indiana disappears every year; overfishing has caused the collapse of many oceanic fisheries; farmers move on to even more marginal land, aggravating an already serious soil erosion problem; and overgrazing is abetting the spread of deserts, which is occurring on 12 percent of the surface of the earth. Furthermore, there is evidence that the global per capita productivity of each of the four natural systems (forests, fisheries, grasslands, and croplands) has peaked and is now declining. There is more evidence indicating that the peak will not be surpassed in the foreseeable future.

AGRICULTURAL LAND

Roughly one tenth of the earth's 13 billion hectares of land surface is cropland. On this land the indigenous forest or grass cover has been replaced with the selected plant species that best serve human needs. Yet the deterioration and loss of the resources essential for agriculture is accelerating and is perhaps the most serious resource problem the world faces.

There are numerous contributing factors: soil erosion, loss of nutrients and compaction of soils, increasing salinization of both irrigated land and water used for irrigation, loss of high-quality cropland to urban development, crop damage due to increasing air and water pollution, extinction of local and wild crop strains needed by plant breeders for improving cultivated varieties, and more frequent and more severe regional water shortages (especially where energy and industrial developments compete for water supplies or where forest losses are heavy and the earth can no longer absorb, store, and regulate the discharge of water).

Turning first to the actual loss of good cropland, urban enroachment is a widespread problem. Cities and industries are often located on a nation's best agricultural land—rich, well-watered alluvial soils in gently sloping river valleys. In the industrialized countries that are members of the Organization for Economic

Cooperation and Development (OECD), the amount of land devoted to urban uses has been increasing twice as fast as population. In Japan, where the spread of industry into former farming areas in the vicinity of large cities reduced the land available for agricultural production by about 6 percent during the 1960s, the situation looks even worse. Canada, the second leading exporter of cereals after the United States, is losing large chunks of its best cropland to urban sprawl and other nonfarm uses.

The limited data available for developing countries point to similar trends. In Egypt, for example, despite efforts to open new lands to agriculture, the total area of irrigated farmland has remained almost unchanged in the past two decades. As fast as additional acres are irrigated with water from the Aswan Dam, old producing lands on the Nile are converted to urban uses. An estimated 26 million hectares of the best cropland along the Nile was being lost each year in the mid 1970s. India projected an increase in the use of land for nonagricultural uses from 16.2 million hectares in 1970 to 26 million hectares by the year 2000.

Soil erosion on remaining cropland is undermining agricultural productivity throughout the world. Certainly not a new phenomenon, it is the high rate of soil reosion that distinguishes the current era.

A particularly worrisome form of erosion is desertification. This does not necessarily mean the creation of Sahara-like sand deserts. Rather it includes a variety of ecological changes that destroy the cover of vegetation and fertile soil in the earth's drier regions, rendering the land useless for range or crops. Principal direct causes are overgrazing, destructive cropping practices, and use of woody plants for fuel.

Global losses to desertification have been estimated at about 6 million hectares a year (an area about the size of Maine), including 32 million hectares of rangeland, 2.5 million hectares of rain-fed cropland, and 125,000 hectares of irrigated farmland. At these estimated rates of desertification, the world's desert areas (now some 800 million hectares) would expand almost 20 percent by 2000. But there is reason to expect that losses to desertification will accelerate as increasing numbers of people in the world's drier regions put more pressures on the land to meet their needs for livestock range, cropland, and fuelwood. The United Nations (UN) has identified about 2 billion hectares of lands where the risk of desertification is "high" or "very high." These lands at risk total about 2.5 times the area now classified as desert.

According to UN estimates, erosion robs Colombia of 426 million tons of fertile topsoil each year, a loss equal to 30 centimeters of soil on 160,000 hectares. Colombia's topsoil is relatively thin, and the nation can ill afford to see it washed away. A UN report on Mexico estimated that 150,000 to 200,000 hectares have been rendered unusable by erosion. In Pakistan, progressive deforestation has led to severe soil erosion and loss of cropland. At some point these losses in Colombia and other severely affected countries may begin to overwhelm the efforts to expand output.

The impact of these trends in loss of cropland and soil erosion is clearly seen in agricultural productivity figures. From the end of World War II until the early 1970s one of the most predictable trends in the world economy was the steady rise in cereal yield per hectare. Between 1950 and 1973 the average worldwide grain yield per hectare moved steadily upward from just under 1.04 tons per hectare to 1.77 tons per hectare (hectare equals 2.47 acres). Beginning in 1974 the trend was interrupted as yields declined somewhat. Experience in the United States closely adhered to this global trend as record yields per hectare occurred in 1971 for wheat and barley and 1972 for corn and sorghum.

Viewed most broadly, the annual rate of increase in grain yield per hectare for the world as a whole was 1.8 percent during the 1950s, 2.5 percent during the 1960s, and 1.5 percent during the 1970s.[2] Though grain yields will continue to rise substantially in many areas of the world and over the remainder of the century on average, it is unlikely that the world as a whole will be able to regain and sustain the 2.5 percent rate of annual increase of the 1960s. Indeed, the grain yield per hectare, like any other biological growth function, is already conforming to the S-shaped growth curve that biologists and agronomists agree it must over the long term.

Since little new land remains to be opened up to agriculture, this downturn in yield per hectare has hit the world food economy hard, contributing to food scarcity and rising food prices. The falloff appears to be the product of several factors. The addition of low-quality land to the cropland base, soaring energy costs, temporary shortages of fertilizer, the shortening of fallow cycles, the diversion of cow dung from fertilizer to fuel uses, and the gradual loss of topsoil through erosion have all helped interrupt the postwar rise in land productivity. While the world demand for food expands at a record rate, the difficulties of raising or, in some situations, even maintaining soil fertility are multiplying. Only by applying ever-larger amounts of fertilizer can many farmers maintain the fertility of their soils. Since the energy used in fertilizer production is becoming more costly, the large rise in crop yields projected by agriculturists for the remainder of this century can no longer be taken for granted.

FORESTS

Global forest trends stand in sharp contrast to the generally favorable domestic forest trends discussed earlier. Indeed, the rapid and wide-ranging disappearance of tropical forests poses a most serious threat to the biosphere.

The **Global 2000 Report** projected that if present trends continue, both forest cover and growing stocks of commercial-size wood in the less developed regions will decline 40 percent by 2000.[3] This statement may be somewhat exaggerated, but most studies point to a very serious problem.

A 1981 Food and Agricultural Organization (FAO) study stated that the tropical deforestation rate is 0.64 percent in Latin America, 0.6l percent in tropical Africa, and 0.60 percent in tropical Asia (about half the rates indicated in the **Global 2000 Report**).[4] An Interagency Task Force on tropical forests reported that tropical forests are in jeopardy.[5] A committee of the National Research Council quite forcefully concluded:

> Even though tropical forests may persist in western Brazil, Amazonia and Central America for another 40 or 50 years, in most other areas it will be reduced much sooner to scattered degraded remnants . . . and to a few parks and reserves.[6]

The Interagency Task Force reported worldwide losses of closed tropical forest at 10 to 20 million hectares (24 to 48 million acres), or 1 to 2 percent per year. (The smaller figure is about the size of Indiana). Deforestation is projected to continue until about 2020, when the total world forest area will stabilize at about 1.8 billion hectares. Most of the loss will occur in the tropical forests of the developing world. About 1.45 billion hectares of forest in the industrialized nations have already stabilized, and about 0.37 billion hectares of forest in the developing countries are physically or economically inaccessible. By 2020 virtually all of the physically accessible forest in the developing countries is expected to have been cut.

The real prices for wood products—fuel wood, sawed lumber, wood panels, paper, wood-based chemicals, and so on—are expected to rise considerably as gross national product (GNP) (and thus also demand) rises and world supplies tighten. In the industrialized nations, the effects may be disruptive but not catastrophic. In the developing countries, however, 90 percent of wood consumption goes for cooking and heating, and wood is a life necessity. Loss of woodlands will force people in many developing countries to pay steeply rising prices for fuelwood and charcoal or to spend much more effort collecting wood—or else to do without.

The severity of the problem unfolding cannot be fully appreciated without looking at the actual experience of some countries. Forests that once covered a third of the total land area of Morocco, Tunisia, and Algeria, for example, had been reduced to scarcely a tenth of their original area by the mid-twentieth century. Despite the major reforestation programs that are under way throughout North Africa, the net loss continues unabated. At least a third of the grassy savannah in sub-Saharan Africa was once forest. More than 70 percent of the forest area the Ivory Coast had at the beginning of the century has already been cleared. In Nigeria the shrinkage of the forests prompted one forester to talk about "timber famine" before the end of the century.

Deforestation threatens all ecological systems and undermines the fertility and stability of soils. Over the past generation, the Indian subcontinent has been progressively deforested; as a result the soil's ability to absorb and hold water has diminished, and flooding has become more frequent and more severe. Deforestation has taken its greatest toll in the Himalayas and in the surrounding foothills where the subcontinent's major river systems—the Indus, the Ganges, and the Brahmaputra—originate. In Nepal it is reported that the destruction of the forests is progressing more rapidly every year and the country is likely to be all but totally denuded by the end of the century. Nearly two thirds of the moist forest has already been converted to other purposes in India, Sri Lanka, and Burma.

In Central America, Honduras has lost from 30 to 40 percent of its forest cover over the past 20 years; at current rates of depletion the country could be entirely denuded within two generations. In a ten-year period Costa Rica lost one third of its forest cover. In Haiti only 9 percent of the original forests remain.

Projections for the next 10 to 20 years are equally startling:

> Virtually all lowland forests of the Philippines, peninsular Malaysia, and most of West Africa seem likely to be logged over by 1990 at the latest. Almost all of Indonesia's lowland forests are scheduled for timber cutting by 2000, one-half by 1990. Bangladesh, Thailand, India, and Sri Lanka could all lose much or most of their forest by 1990. Central America's moist forests could all but disappear by 1990.[7]

Many industrialized countries face serious problems, though they are of a different nature and not as critical. Nevertheless, Europe is expected to have a deficit of about 10 billion cubic feet in 2000, and Japan already imports 66 percent of its wood. Japan is now protecting its steeper slopes from deforestation, but this has required large imports of timber from Southeast Asia and elsewhere. Western Europe's reasonable balance between the ecological need for forests and other land uses is a balance maintained in part by large imports of wood and wood products, principally from Scandinavia, the Soviet Union, and tropical Africa.[8] Two UN studies have forecast that expanding demand for timber products will soon be running ahead of what Sweden will have available for cutting. Since Sweden supplies 30 percent of Europe's timber and 60 percent of its pulp, the repercussions for Europe's construction and paper industries could be severe.[9]

The resulting adverse effects of deforestation on other renewable resources—notably water, air, and plant and animal species—are numerous and growing increasingly serious.[10] With regard to water, deforestation—especially in South Asia, the Amazon basin, and central Africa—will destabilize water flows, leading to siltation of streams, reservoirs behind hydroelectric dams, and irrigation works; depletion of groundwater; intensified flooding; and aggravated water shortages during dry periods. In South and Southeast Asia, approximately 1 billion people live in heavily farmed alluvial basins and valleys that depend on forested mountain watersheds for their water. If present trends continue, forests in these regions will be reduced by about half in 2000, and erosion, siltation, and erratic stream flows will seriously affect food production.

There is also serious concern among some scientists that destruction of forests may change the world's climate in ways highly unfavorable to the human species. Two kind of effects are of interest. First, alterations in the global climate might result from changes in the earth's *albedo* — that is, the reflection of light and heat from the earth's surface — when light-absorbing forests are removed. The heat balance of the earth would change, producing consequent changes in wind and rainfall patterns. The second effect involves the carbon dioxide buildup problem, examined in the "atmosphere and climate section".

Finally, species extinction is an extremely serious impact. Tropical forests are enormously diverse. Whereas a European forest typically contains 5 or 10 species of tree per hectare (2.5 acres), a tropical moist forest usually has 100 to 150 different tree species — in addition to a rich diversity of other plants and animals.[11] At the same time, these species may be of very limited geographic distribution, and because they have no means of wide dispersal, once they are gone there is no recolonization from outside. The broad context is that between 0.5 million and 2 million species — 10 to 20 percent of all species on earth — could be extinguished by 2000, according to one estimate.[12] One half to two thirds of these extinctions would result from the clearing or degradation of tropical forests. Insect, other invertebrate, and plant species — many of them unclassified and unexamined by scientists — will account for most of the losses. The potential value of this genetic reservoir is immense.

WATER

All projections point to rapidly increasing demands for fresh water through the end of the century. Increases of at least 200 to 300 percent in world water withdrawals are expected over the 1975–2000 period. Regional water shortages and deterioration of water quality, already serious in many parts of the world, are likely to become worse by 2000.

By far the largest part of the increase is for irrigation. The United Nations has estimated that water needed for irrigation, which accounted for 70 percent of human uses of water in 1967, will double by 2000.[13] Moreover, irrigation is a highly consumptive use: that is, much of the water withdrawn for this purpose is not available for immediate reuse because it evaporates, or it is transpired by plants, or it becomes salinated.

Heightened demands will most likely increase the already fierce competition for water among countries with common river systems. One only needs to review recent history to see the potential for conflict. Competition for water among countries with common river systems has become increasingly fierce. Protracted negotiations were required to allocate the waters of the Indus River between India and Pakistan; conflicts between India and Bangladesh over the right to use the Ganges River surfaced in 1976. Competition is also keen between Israel and the Arab countries for the waters of the Jordan River.

Much of the increased demand for water will be in the developing countries of Africa, South Asia, the Middle East, and Latin America, where in many areas fresh water for human consumption and irrigation is already in short supply. Several nations in these areas will be approaching their maximum developable water supply by 2000, and they will find it quite expensive to develop the water remaining. Many developing countries will also suffer destabilization of water supplies following extensive loss of forests. In the industrialized countries, competition among different users of water — for increasing food production, creating new energy systems (such as production of synthetic fuels from coal and shale), increasing power generation, expanding food production, and increasing needs of other industry — will aggravate water shortages in many areas.

The bottom line, however, is the impact on irrigation worldwide, for the prospect of adequately feeding the future population is pinned to the prospect of expanding the area irrigated by large-scale river systems and wells. The chance that more rivers can be harnessed appears much smaller in the fourth quarter of this century than it did in the third. The easiest extensive irrigation projects to build — whether in China, India, the Soviet Union, the Middle East, Africa, or North America — have already been completed. The irrigation potential of most of the world's major rivers, including the Yellow, the Indus, the Ganges, the Colorado, and the Egyptian share of the Nile, has largely been realized. The Mekong and the Amazon remain unexploited, but the latter's vast width and broad floodplains make it virtually impossible to harness.

Opportunities for expanding well irrigation are limited by the extent of underground water supplies and by the rising cost of the fuels needed to operate pumps. Unused potential may be greatest in the Gangetic and Indus floodplains in the Indian subcontinent, where underground water supplies are both abundant and close to the surface. In the United States well irrigation in the western Great Plains and in the Southwest has expanded rapidly, often to such an extent that water tables are now dropping. Thus, while the world's irrigated area expanded by 2.6 percent annually between 1950 and 1975, it will probably grow at less than half that rate for the remainder of this century.

The oceans that cover two thirds of the earth's surface constitute an integral part of humanity's life-support system, supplying both food and oxygen. They have generally been considered too vast for humans to harm. Thus, they were regarded as a convenient, limitless receptacle for wastes. Experience and greater understanding are teaching us that despite their vastness the oceans' natural capacity to receive, decompose, and recycle wastes has limits. Furthermore, the scale of human activity is now such that it can damage the seas irrevocably.

The oceans have become the planet's ultimate waste receptacle, the passive recipient of staggering amounts of industrial, agricultural, and municipal wastes. Hydrocarbon pollution — the legacy of offshore drilling, routine oil tanker operations, and the growing number of wrecked oil tankers — is growing rapidly. The amount of oil spilled from tankers in 1979 was more that 2.5 times any previous year. There were 65 incidents involving tankers greater than 6,000 tons deadweight and about 724,000 metric tons of oil. Spoils from the dredging of rivers and harbors — often containing heavy metals, persistent organic chemicals, and other toxic chemicals — are also dumped. Several European countries (principally Britain, Belgium, the Netherlands, and Switzerland) currently dump low-level radioactive wastes at a site in the North Atlantic. Japan anticipates beginning ocean dumping of such wastes, and the United States is evaluating the potential impacts of ocean disposal. The volume and types of wastes dumped, particularly toxic materials and radioactive wastes, clearly dictate the need for understanding the effects of these wastes and for pursuing continued and expanded international cooperation.

ATMOSPHERE AND CLIMATE

The three main global atmospheric problems that have received considerable attention in the popular press in the United States in recent years are carbon dioxide (CO_2) buildup (the greenhouse effect), acid rain, and depletion of the ozone layer. What is known is that these trends are occurring. What is not known, thus making these issues extremely controversial and at times emotional, is how serious the threat is and the time period involved.

Looking first at what is known, the flow of CO_2 to the atmosphere is intensified through burning fossil fuels, clearing forests, cultivating land. As a consequence, the amount of CO_2 in the atmosphere is increasing, probably about 4 percent every ten years. Atmospheric CO_2 causes a greenhouse effect by allowing shortwave solar radiation to pass through to the earth while partially trapping outgoing infrared heat radiated by the earth. It now is 17 percent higher than its pre–Industrial Revolution level.

Present concern is centered on the plans for rapid expansion of coal as a primary substitute source for energy, not only in the United States but globally. If such expansion occurred, atmospheric CO_2 could double by the year 2050, which in turn could lead to an increase in average global surface temperatures of about 3°C and increase the winter average in the polar regions as much as 7°C to 10°C.[14] An emerging body of opinion holds that this could result in a rapid melting of the Greenland and Antarctic ice caps, which in turn could lead to a five-meter rise in sea level, covering many low-lying land areas and inundating the major coastal cities. Precipitation and growing seasons for crops could be greatly altered, possibly disrupting world agriculture; one result might be persistent drought in grain belts such as the midwestern United States.

The ultimate confounding problem is that scientific proof of the warming of the earth may come after the time has passed when action can be taken to reverse the trend. We would do well to heed the warning of a recent government study: "It is the sense of the scientific community that carbon dioxide from the unrestrained combustion of fossil fuels is potentially the most important environmental issue facing mankind."[15]

Acid rain is recognized as the other most serious global environmental problem associated with fossil fuel combustion. It is a major problem on both sides of the Atlantic and in Japan. In the eastern half of the United States, the acidity of rainfall appears to have increased about 50-fold during the past 25 years.

Although insufficient knowledge exists concerning the explicit causes and the long-reaching effects of acid rain, some effects are quite clear. In Scandinavia, southern Canada, and the northeastern part of the United States, many lakes and estuaries have experienced depletions of fish life, and in some cases, they have become totally devoid of fish. Such losses are an indication of major upsets in ecological balances, which may be more far-reaching than the recreational resource loss. In addition, loss of crop productivity and forest yields due to acid rain may be prevalent. Acid rain also damages steel and stone structures as well as works of art. Many of these effects may be permanent. Acid rain is a prime example of an area requiring international cooperation. Canada and the United States signed a memorandum in August 1980 indicating both governments' intention to negotiate a cooperative agreement on air pollution crossing their borders. Progress, however, has been very slow. Clearly, coordination and cooperation among their respective agencies and organizations need to be improved.

A thoughtful overall perspective on this issue was given in a National Academy of Sciences report, released in September 1981 by its Committee on the Atmosphere and the Biosphere. It observed that "emissions of sulfur and nitrogen oxides at current or accelerated rates, in the face of clear evidence of serious hazard to human health and to the biosphere, will be extremely risky from a long-term economic standpoint as well as from the standpoint of biosphere protection."[16] It therefore concluded that the "picture is disturbing enough to merit prompt tightening of restrictions on atmospheric emissions from fossil fuels and other large sources such as metal smelters and cement manufacture."[17]

The ozone problem involves the release of chlorofluorocarbons, which convert some of the ozone in the stratosphere into oxygen. Since stratospheric ozone filters out most of the ultraviolet radiation in sunlight, a decrease in its concentration would permit more ultraviolet radiation to reach the earth's surface. The most widely discussed effect of ozone depletion is an increased incidence of skin cancer, but damage to food crops would also be significant and might actually prove to be the most serious ozone-related problem. Concern has increased in the past years owing to two 1979 reports from the National Academy of Sciences projecting that continued production and release of the chemicals at the 1977 rate will lead to an eventual 16.5 percent depletion of 1977 levels of stratospheric ozone.[18] This was more than twice the depletion reported in a 1976 report by the same panel. If chlorofluorocarbon releases were to increase 7 percent per year between 1980 and 2000, the eventual depletion of ozone would probably exceed 30 percent. The bottom line is that growth in production and use of chlorofluorocarbons, which is expected to occur if controls are not established in countries other than the United States, will lead to major disturbances of the stratosphere.

MINERALS

The trends for nonfuel minerals show steady increases in demand and consumption. The global demand for and consumption of most major nonfuel mineral commodities is projected to increase 3 to 5 percent annually, slightly more than doubling by 2000.[19] Consumption of all major steel-making mineral commodities is projected to increase at least 3 percent annually. Consumption of all mineral commodities for fertilizer production is projected to grow at more than 3 percent annually, with consumption of phosphate rock growing at 5.2 percent per year — the highest growth rate projected for any of the major nonfuel mineral commodities. The nonferrous metals have widely varying projected growth rates; the growth rate for aluminum, 4.3 percent per year, is the largest.

The projections suggest that the developing countries' share of nonfuel mineral use will increase only modestly. Over the 1971–75 period, Latin America, Africa, and Asia used 7 percent of the world's aluminum production, 9 percent of the copper, and 12 percent of the iron ore. The three quarters of the world's population living in these regions in 2000 are projected to use only 8 percent of aluminum production, 13 percent of copper production, and 17 percent of iron ore production. The one quarter of the world's population that inhabits industrial countries in projected to continue absorbing more than three fourths of the world's nonfuel minerals production.

The problem with such aggregate figures is that they mask important differences among developing nations on the exporter side of mineral markets. Not all developing nations have been equally favored with abundant natural resources. The majority have extremely small or nonexistent mineral-extracting sectors. It is estimated that 61 out of 103 developing nations do not have substantial mineral deposits. About 90 percent of developing nations' exports of fuels and minerals are accounted for by countries containing less than one-fourth of the population of the less developed world. Thus, the fortunes of less developed countries do not vary uniformly with increasing or decreasing nonfuel mineral prices. Most of them have little or no role as exporters in minerals markets.

The Third World may be viewed in terms of three groups of countries having different mineral interests and prospects. The top tier of nouveau riche oil-exporting countries is interested mainly in maintaining and increasing petroleum prices. But whether they are financially willing to support price-increasing cartels in nonfuel mineral markets remains unclear, since very few petroleum exporters also export nonfuel minerals in significant quantities. The second tier of developing countries, composed of a small number of nonfuel mineral exporters, favors dramatic increases in prices for their exports. But such increases would be of no benefit to oil-exporting countries or to the agrarian developing countries that make up the bulk of the Third World. Any increases in the price of nonfuel minerals would also benefit many industrial exporters, and those who are our exporters would pass increased costs through in the form of higher prices for industrial goods. For the bottom layer of developing countries, the so-called Fourth World, increases in any mineral prices would be another serious economic setback.

4

ECONOMIC TRANSFORMATION

The past 15 years have been years of extraordinary economic difficulties for the United States, as for most of the industrialized world. Inflation remained high, economic growth slowed, the rate of productivity improvement shrunk to very low levels, trade imbalances increased, and unemployment reached and remained at stubbornly high levels. These factors, combined with eroding markets and constraints on capital availability, have raised questions about the vitality of the United States' core industrial sector. In addition, what compounds present-day concerns and fears is that the standard cure for such ills — demand management policies — seems to have lost its potency.

The end result has been great frustration on the part of the American public and a disturbing uncertainty concerning the future. Citizens have seen the rise in their standard of living slow down significantly, halt, or even reverse, an unprecedented development in the post–World War II period. They have become concerned over the possibility that the United States is on the road to becoming a second-rate world power. They want the decline to be halted and then reversed.

To accomplish this, we need to understand both today's economic realities and the likely realities of 1990. As obvious as this may seem, too many government policy makers either assume the world is the same as when they were growing up or else try to force economic reality into an ideological mold with a "let's skip the facts" attitude. Nostalgic or doctrinaire approaches will not work. We have to deal with the facts as they are, not as we would wish them to be.

More than half a century ago, the leading economist of the era, John Maynard Keynes, wrote: "We do not dance even yet to a new tune. But change is in the air." In 1926 change certainly was in the air, and it blew in with a vengeance in 1929. And when the changed economic conditions arrived, it was Keynes who set not only his native England but most of the Western world dancing to a new economic tune.

Today change is once again in the air, and a new economic tune is needed. We cannot rely on traditional economic assumptions, dogmas, and practices to get us the type of strong economic performance and increased standard of living we all desire. We must forge our economic strategy with clear goals in mind and in full knowledge of the tremendously powerful winds of change buffeting our economy. These "winds" will profoundly alter our patterns of economic growth, which in turn will significantly alter environmental and natural resource trends.

The United States is in the midst of two fundamental long-run structural changes that are transforming both economic performance and the economic arena. Domestically, we are shifting from an economy based primarily on basic manufacturing and heavy industry to one based on information, communications, high technology, and services. Globally, we have increasingly become part of an international economy in which new actors on the world stage influence domestic economic performance to an unparalleled degree. In short we are experiencing simultaneously an *information revolution* and an *interdependence revolution*. The key economic challenge of the 1980s is to restore economic growth by capitalizing on, rather than resisting, these two fundamental economic changes.

DOMESTIC TRANSFORMATION

Without much fanfare until recently, our economy has been shifting from one based primarily on heavy industry and basic manufacturing — steel, cars, and so on — to one based on information, communications, high technology, and services. More U.S. workers are now engaged in generating, processing, distributing, and analyzing information than are employed in argiculture, mining, construction, and manufacturing goods combined.

This revolution — involving explosive innovation in computers, communications, telecommunications, and microprocessors — is the single most powerful economic force for change in the world today. As it surrounds the globe with instantaneous, comprehensive and continuous communication, both our international competitive position and some of our basic institutions and policies will be tested. The real issue is how to make this revolution work for us.

Certainly, the information revolution is loaded with opportunities. Just as the Industrial Revolution dramatically expanded human physical capacities, so the information revolution magnifies mental capacities. Unlike the Industrial Revolution, which depended on finite resources such as oil and iron, the new information age will be driven by a limitless resource: our inexhaustible ability to generate knowledge.

Moreover, whereas the Industrial Revolution made available and employed vast amounts of mechanical energy, the information revolution is extremely sparing of energy and materials. The application of "intelligence" alone can help to save evergy. For example, electronic engine controls using sensors and microprocessors will help the auto industry meet government requirements for increased gasoline mileage in passenger cars. Telecommunications can help conserve resources. Over the last decade a reduction of only 1 percent of U.S. business travel by air and automobile would have saved roughly 25 million barrels of fuel. Savings of this kind could easily be made through the use of new business information systems now appearing.

The general principle to keep in mind is that there are different ways to apply energy to a productive task, some more wise than others. As technology advances and as we learn more about how the world is constructed, the potential role of information and knowledge becomes correspondingly greater. For instance, the fact that distance is no longer a barrier to communication is not due to a substitution of capital for labor but rather to a substitution of one kind of capital for another: of information-intensive capital for energy-intensive capital.

Most generally, widespread introduction of information technologies into traditional manufacturing industries has the potential to increase productivity on a scale never before conceivable and to transform these industries into modern, efficient producers competitive in world markets. Unless this occurs, many of our traditional manufacturing industries will be unable to compete with foreign manufacturers, whose lower wages and modern plants provide a considerable cost advantage.

There is no question: We are entering a new era, one with unlimited potential. But our future depends on embracing not only the new technologies and the opportunity they provide but the responsibilities they bring as well.

In particular, we must deal forthrightly with the fact that the transformation our economy is undergoing will affect U.S. jobs and jobholders on an unprecedented scale. We will see a radical restructuring of work, as current work skills are devalued and new ones created at an ever-increasing rate. As many as 45 million existing jobs could be affected by factory and office automation, and much of that impact will occur in the next 20 years. The well-being of today's workers and those entering the work force in the 1980s depends on finding effective ways to adjust to this upheaval.

The evolution in information technology itself and the changing labor force composition have simply paved the way for the revolution in the applications of the technology that is just now beginning. The precise nature of the profound and pervasive changes of the next 20 years can be only dimly perceived. What is a virtual certainty is that the information age will change forever the way an entire nation works, plays, and even thinks.

Two major features of the information revolution deserve separate and more detailed attention because they are vital components of the domestic economic transformation: the United States' five subeconomies and the transforming labor force.

In addition to the overall shift in the underlying economic base, there is the complicating fact that instead of having a national or aggregate economy the United States really has five subeconomies: traditional manufacturing, agriculture, energy, high-technology, and services. The first three have existed throughout this century, while the latter two are creatures of the information revolution. As should be expected, having five economies, instead of one, complicates economic decisions greatly.

First, the five do not experience recoveries equally, nor do they decline together in recessions. Each subeconomy has a life of its own because each is driven by unique forces. The implications of this are far-reaching. Traditional indicators (such as GNP and the unemployment rate) no longer provide a very accurate picture of economic performance. This in turn means that sole reliance on broad macroeconomic policies, such as changes in the money supply, is not likely to solve the problems of each subeconomy. The requirements of ailing basic industries, after all, are substantially different from those of the energy and high-technology industries.

Another major impact resulting from this segmented economy is the serious problem of regional imbalance. Generally industries with the healthiest growth tend to be concentrated in the Sunbelt and the West, while those with the poorest growth and greatest difficulties are concentrated in the Northeast and Midwest. Such differences in growth rates among sectors and regions is not cause for alarm in and of itself. Indeed, what Joseph Schumpeter called "the process of creative destruction" is a vital, natural part of any growing, technologically innovative economy. The problem today is that the pace of dislocation is now so fast it is generating new tensions not only among regions but among industries as well.

A number of concurrent fundamental trends are transforming the labor force. These "labor market facts of life" are:

- We will be experiencing much slower labor force growth in the last half of the 1980s;
- We have experienced and will continue to experience, a revolution in the composition of our labor force — principally the tremendous influx of women; and
- We will be experiencing an occupational upheaval of unprecedented magnitude in the coming decade.

Sheer demographics drives the first trend, while the latter two are directly related to the information revolution.

The first trend involves the straightforward projection that labor force growth will drop from recent rates of over 2 percent to less than 1.0 percent in 1990. In other words there will be fewer than half the number of job seekers each year, which means lower unemployment pressures as the decade wears on. Another perspective is that today's workers will constitute over 90 percent of the work force in 1990 and over 75 percent in the year 2000.

The second fact of life is that women have become a major part of the labor force. Spurred on by information and service jobs, their labor force participation rate increased from 37 percent in 1960 to over 50 percent in 1980. Of the baby-boom generation, nearly 70 percent are in the labor force. Most striking of all, fully 46 percent of women with preschool children are working — up from only 31 percent in 1970. A large majority, 63 percent, of women with children aged 6 to 17 are in the labor force. In all, almost 17 million mothers are working or looking for jobs. Moreover, the entry of women into the labor force is projected to continue. Women will make up fully two thirds of the labor force growth between now and 1990. By 2000 a *majority* of workers between the ages of 16 and 24 will be women for the first time in our history.

Third, there will be massive occupational upheaval in the next two decades. The process of displacement of manufacturing workers has been taking place for some time, but it will accelerate dramatically in the latter half of the 1980s. Already the percentage of manufacturing workers in the total work force has gone from 34 percent in 1950 to 23 percent in 1979. As to the future, Peter Drucker makes this dramatic projection:

> It is predictable and practically certain that, 25 years from now, the proportion of the American labor force engaged in blue-collar manufacturing work will not be much larger than the proportion now engaged in farming — that is, less than 10 and not much more than 5 percent of the total labor force.[1]

Even if he is only half right, you say good-bye to 5 to 7.5 million manufacturing jobs. To put this in a current-day perspective, the 300,000 recently displaced auto workers will be multiplied by 16 to 25 times for manufacturing workers in general — unless these workers are redirected toward, and retrained for, new jobs.

Workers who lose their jobs to the new technologies may find fewer places to go. In the last decade the service sector held many opportunities for displaced factory workers: almost 7 million new jobs between 1970 and 1977. Today, however, many of those same jobs (in banking, insurance, retailing, and secretarial and clerical work) are the microprocessor's principal target.

The news, however, is not all bad. Occupational upheaval means the creation of new jobs and new types of jobs as well as the destruction of old jobs. For example, it is projected that nearly 1.5 million jobs will be available in 1990 in three resource/environmental job categories: energy technician, hazardous waste management technician, and materials utilization technician.[2]

GLOBAL TRANSFORMATION

The phrase *global interdependence* has floated around in economic discussions for decades. It was brought down to earth by three new actors, each of whom made a forceful debut on the world stage in the 1970s: Japan, which has emerged as our dominant competitor in world markets; the newly industrialized countries, such as Brazil, Taiwan, and Mexico, now beginning to compete with the United States in world markets as well as to offer new markets; and the Organization of Petroleum Exporting Countries (OPEC), whose control over oil supplies threatens our economic prosperity and our foreign policy independence.

These recent developments have made the life of each American increasingly dependent on decisions made elsewhere. They also mean that our own economic decisions have global consequences. The result is a substantial reduction in the effectiveness of purely domestic policies on economic activity — in short, a reduction in our sovereignty over our own economy.

The transformation is particularly evident in world trade. Virtually all U.S. industries, including those that still generate tremendous trade surpluses, have been steadily losing their share of the world market. Look at exports to developing countries: the U.S. share fell from 28.3 to 22.1 percent between 1970 and 1978; Japan's rose from 21.8 to 26.1 percent. Meanwhile, imports are cutting into the dominance that U.S. industry has long maintained in domestic markets. From 1960 to 1979 the share of the U.S. market taken by American-made cars went from 95 percent to 60 percent; shoes, from 98 to 63 percent; textile machinery, from 93 to 55 percent; and calculators, adding machines, radios, and televisions, from 95 percent to about 50 percent.

Such facts make clear that the U.S. trade policy for the rest of the 1980s and the 1990s must be shaped around a fundamental imperative: The "market" is now the global market, and if we are going to make it over the long haul as economic leaders, we have to pursue competitive positions in this new marketplace aggressively. Equally important is that we move ahead thoughtfully. This is no little sideshow we are dealing with. The wealth and welfare of all nations is at stake to say nothing of the livelihood of their people. A surgeon's scalpel is needed more than a bludgeon.

Clearly, whatever actions we take in the international arena — trade, international debt, exchange rate, and the like — must be guided by clear understanding of four central facts regarding the global economy and the U.S. position in it.

The first and foremost fact is that the global economy is precariously balanced on a knife-edge with a dangerous tilt toward international economic disintegration. Basically, the choice is which road should we follow: pushing further for an open world economy operating on, and governed by, the multilateral framework of the General Agreement on Tariffs and Trade (GATT) or pushing for bilateral or sectoral balance through unilateral retaliatory means and general protectionist measures. This is one of the most basic economic decisions we as a country must make. It is also the most important decision influencing the future prosperity of not only this country but of all countries in the world.

The United States as the world's largest trader has it in its own best interest, to say nothing of the best interests of all nations, to continue the push for a more open world economy. Unfortunately, many industrialized countries are moving in precisely the opposite direction. Economic nationalism has paradoxically reasserted itself even as the world becomes increasingly interdependent. European producers of autos, television sets, synthetic fibers, and steel have all pushed for import restraints, and Japan remains the hardest market for an outsider to crack. The United States is far from exempt. The list of U.S. industries seeking government protection from imports includes makers of everything from cars and golf carts to nuts and bolts. Going even further, in some quarters there is a definite push for movement toward economic isolationism.

We have only to look back half a century to realize what the last major experiment in economic nationalism, isolationism, and retaliation gave us. Historical experience demonstrates that unilateral retaliatory or protectionist actions by one country tend to set off a vicious cycle of protectionist responses by that country's trade partners. Hence, protectionism breeds protectionism. Let us be wise enough and vigilant enough to prevent history from repeating itself.

Fact number two is that the U.S. trade position is a complex mosaic, with intermingling strengths and weaknesses. It is unfortunate that it is usually the weaknesses — our trade problems — that receive all the attention, thereby distorting the overall picture.

The weakness in our trading posture centers on the long-term deterioration of our merchandise trade account vis-à-vis other countries.

The U.S. balance on merchandise trade has been steadily worsening: it was in surplus most of the 1960s, dropped to even by the late 1960s, and showed deficits for seven years in the 1970s with skyrocketing deficits for the last four years of the decade. In consumer goods U.S. trade went from –7.0 billion in 1970 to –30.2 billion in 1979. In manufactured goods the U.S. global market share in 1980 was declining for 71 percent of 102 manufactured commodities (compared with 26 percent for Japan and 24 percent for West Germany). In markets shared with major foreign competitors, the United States suffered market share losses in 14 out of 17 top export commodities during the 1960s and all 17 in the 1970s. These trends in the trade of goods (as opposed to services) are what lies behind the frustrating fact that even as we move ahead, we fall behind. While U.S. exports increased from 4 percent of our GNP in 1970 to 8 percent today, our share of the total world export market declined from 15 percent to 12 percent.

There have been two fundamental and important reasons for our merchandise trade deficits of recent years. The first is no mystery to anyone: the enormous increase in our oil import bills in the 1970s. From 1973 to 1981 this bill jumped from $8 billion to $78 billion. If we exclude our oil imports, the United States had a substantial merchandise trade surplus in each year from 1977 to 1981, reaching approximately $50 billion in 1981.

The other major cause is even more important, yet it has remained largely hidden: the serious deterioration in U.S. price competitiveness. With respect to West Germany and Japan, the deterioration was 50 percent or more in the 1979–81 period. This fact of the overvalued dollar and undervalued yen is the fundamental cause of our huge trade deficit with Japan. Measured against all trading nations, the average decline in U.S. price competitiveness during that three-year period was around 25 percent. This hurts our trade position tremendously, because every percentage point of competitive deterioration is likely to produce an adverse swing of $2 to $3 billion in the trade accounts. In short the dollar had become too strong, our exports too expensive.

Fortunately, our strengths are also considerable. When all relevant trade accounts are taken together (which means adding to merchandise trade our trade in services and return on foreign investments), the United States enjoyed a surplus from 1979 to 1981. Services alone have enjoyed $30 to $40 billion surpluses in recent years, a surplus figure also matched by high technology in recent years.

This overall surplus position was not something enjoyed by either Germany or Japan.

Moreover, while we had a $16 billion trade deficit with Japan in 1981, we also enjoyed a trade surplus of $6 billion with the Netherlands, $4 billion with Mexico, and $3.5 billion with Belgium. What this indicates is that individual bilateral trade balances do not provide an accurate reflection of U.S. trade performance.

Fact number three is that the United States' economic contest is principally with Japan. Sure there are many other key contestants (including newly industrialized countries that are coming on strong), but the battle for economic leadership really boils down to the one contestant. This contest began in earnest around 1970 and will probably be decided around 1990. Japan has gained considerably on us in the past 12 years, and if that gap closing continues, it will be by us before we know it.

Whether this occurs depends on what happens in the high-technology field. The signs are not good. Japan has made the high-technology commitment, and the resources and projects are already operating. The Japanese are poised to blow by us here, just as they have done in every field they have concentrated on in the last 20 years, from consumer electronics and cameras through ship building, steel, and automobiles.

The fourth and final fact is that trade policy and our global economic stake are equally as important to our national security as our national defense posture. One without a strong other is a false security. There are a number of ways to view this interrelationship. One is that building up and supporting a strong military comes much more easily under a healthy, growing economy than a stagnant one. The last two years attest vividly to that fact. At a much deeper level the real ongoing battle with the Soviet Union is taking place in the economic trenches where countries are either drawn closer to the United States or repelled farther away by how we treat them economically. Thus our greatest national defense may be taking the offense on drawing an increasing number of countries into our camp through long-run economic relationships. Finally, a buoyant world economy in which the fruits of prosperity are widely shared may be our best guarantee of national security. A thriving, tightly interwoven global economy is much less likely to experience wars than a stagnant, each nation-for-itself world. Again, the experience of the 1930s attests to this fact.

To conclude, the global economic situation is greatly complicated and made precarious by the basic disjuncture between politics, which is national, and economics, which is international. Economic and industrial policies are made mainly by national governments. Yet most of the industries to which they apply operate in an international market. In short, economic interdependence is increasingly at odds with political systems rooted in the nation-state.

This is a dangerous development if it results in narrow nationalism and its concomitant mercantilism and protectionism, the primary threats to the future economic well-being of mankind.

Thus the fundamental issue we face in the international economic arena is this: Will the world continue to move toward economic cooperation, erasing the economic barriers between countries and encouraging trade, investment, and competition, or will it revert to nationalism and mercantilism, raising walls between countries and limiting trade and communication? The economic well-being of literally hundreds of millions of people hangs in the balance.

II
The Theory

5

NATURAL RESOURCES IN
CONVENTIONAL ECONOMIC THEORY

Natural resources have had quite a roller coaster–type ride in conventional economic theory. The early classical economists (Smith, Ricardo, and so on) placed natural resources at the center of their analyses. In the late nineteenth century, with the rise of the marginalist school of economic thought, they fell into a state of benign neglect, a state that has generally prevailed throughout the past century. There have been relatively few resource economist specialists, and by and large the economics profession as a whole has taken its cues from them. Hence, in the last two decades when resource and environmental problems have come to the fore, virtually all economists have accepted the "no-need-to-worry" conclusions concerning resource availability coming from the resource economists, particularly the writing of Harold Barnett and Chandler Morse.[1] Such optimism was almost a foregone conclusion, based both on the general societal belief that technological solutions would always be at hand and on the economists' reliance on the market. The main elements of the conventional theory will be presented in this chapter, while the critique of the economist's perspective and methodology will follow in Chapter 6.

LAND: THE FORGOTTEN FACTOR
IN THE ECONOMIC TRIAD

Most Americans, if asked what were the key factors in their country's tremendous economic growth over the past century, would most likely include in their answers the opening of the frontier and cheap and abundant natural resources and energy. Most individuals asked to recite what they learned in a principles of economics course would likely remember that the three factors of production are land, labor, and capital.

The answers are "obvious," yet sometime during the nineteenth century practicing economists in fact began to leave *land* (broadly defined as natural resources and the physical environment) out of the analytical picture. Beginning with the rise of the marginalist school of economic thought in the 1870s, economists have constructed, examined, and refined numberless forms of production functions that consisted solely of labor and capital. As Nicholas Georgescu-Roegen has pointed out: "On paper, one can write a production function any way one likes, without regard to dimensions or to other physical constraints."[2] James Tobin and William Nordhaus, two leading mainstream economists, also acknowledge this neglect by economists: "The prevailing standard model of growth . . . is basically a two-factor model in which production depends only on labor and reproducible capital. Land and resources, the third member of the classical triad, have generally been dropped."[3]

Using more poetic phrasing, Bertrand de Jouvenel, the French philosopher and social critic, has scored a similar point about growth theory: "What could be more angelic than the Theory of Growth, of a Growth which can proceed forever on a straight path through ether."[4] He claims that *angelic* characterizes the whole of modern economics, for it has become "bodyless, immaterial," a far cry from what it was in its classical days, from Adam Smith to Marx. Smith, for example, was interested in coal, noting that manufacturers were sited in the neighborhood of coalfields because indoor work called for heating the workrooms. De Jouvenel calls this "concrete vision"; many contemporary economists would regard it as "intellectual slumming."

Contemporary economists have continued, with only a few exceptions, the marginalists' tradition of neglecting the third factor of production. There is no discussion of or even reference to, energy in the most widely used principles of economics textbooks prior to 1973. It has only been in the past decade that the authors of these texts have begun inserting chapters on the environment or natural resources, and even then these usually appear at the end along with other special or miscellaneous topics. The definitive study on sources of

U.S. economic growth, **Accounting for United States Economic Growth, 1929–69,** does not even mention energy or natural resources as a contributing source.[5] The current methodology of economics ignores man's dependence on the natural world.

Today economic theory studies the allocation of scarce resources among competing ends, assuming that resources, personal tastes, and technology are given. Economists, concerned with achieving high economic and productivity growth, or equitable distribution, or low unemployment and inflation rates (or at least with explaining why such worthy goals are not achieved), show little or no regard for evolutionary processes, the dissipation of energy, or the depletion of resources. These aspects of the economic process are considered, if at all, as "externalities" — that is, as costs or benefits that are "external" to the theory.

Perhaps the most obvious example is in regard to pollution. Past failure to apply the market principle to the environment has given the wrong signals for investment and economic growth efforts. We treated as free natural elements such as air and water that really were not free. We were, in effect, subsidizing various goods, which resulted in their overproduction. Economic theory has not developed a conceptual basis for assigning value to natural systems. Natural systems, whose services to human societies are usually not purchased in the market like other commodities and services, have been considered external to the economy. Recent efforts to quantify natural value have spoken of the need to "internalize" natural systems, that is, to make them visible to market-pricing mechanisms.

Natural systems provide many services — maintenance of land and river forms, degradation of wastes, maintenance of soil structure, and maintenance of clean air and water — sometimes collectively called *public service functions*. These functions enter the market because they are the basis of our existence. However, we seldom calculate their value, and when we do, it usually is only after they have been degraded by human activity.

Most mainstream macroeconomists by and large have tended to ignore the growing worldwide scarcities of matter and energy and the increasing pressures on the biosphere. This remains true despite the fact that slow growth, declining productivity, and high inflation — the problems that have so thoroughly frustrated conventional economists — have their roots in that growing scarcity.

This virtually complete neglect would seem difficult to explain, particularly since so much of classical economics dealt with questions related to land. The primary explanation is that since industrialization brought labor and capital together in entirely new ways, enabling undreamed-of production to take place and raising important theoretical questions, theoretical development and analysis naturally flowed in this direction. The massive infusion of fuel and nonfuel minerals providing the basis for such a dynamic industrial thrust went almost unnoticed since their supply was ensured and their cost negligible compared with the other two factors.

Thereafter, optimistic economists generally accepted the view that the same factors that were responsible for relaxing materials constraints in the past would continue. For example, Hendrik Houthakker has observed that "the ancient concern about the depletion of natural resources no longer rests on any firm theoretical basis."

Another explanation has to do with the internal development of the discipline — with economics' intellectual underpinning. A mechanistic epistomology was inherited uncritically from the neoclassical founders for whom economics was "the mechanics of utility and self-interest" (as W. Stanley Jevons proudly professed).[6] Economists argued that "economic equilibrium" and the concept of static equilibrium in mechanics were formally identical. Absolute irreversibility (without any qualitative change) constituted the basis of both states. The vision of the economic process as a self-sustaining, circular affair, as portrayed graphically in virtually all introductory texts, naturally contained no room for consideration of a diminishing natural resource base.

THE CONVENTIONAL MARKET APPROACH OF RESOURCE ECONOMISTS

Most resource economists have taken a very narrow view of resources, focusing primarily on nonrenewable mineral resources to the virtual exclusion of energy, the environment, and all renewable resources. Their work has centered on the themes of scarcity and depletion, and their conclusions have entered into mainstream economics largely unquestioned.

Their economic view of depletion has been quite different than the physical view, which has asked: how long will it be before certain resources are exhausted, before we "run out"? Since the earth is finite, the quantity of a particular mineral is physically limited, and the total available supply of any mineral is a fixed stock. Demand, on the other hand, is a flow variable; it continues year in and year out. Sooner or later demand has to consume the available supply. The end is likely to come sooner rather than later because demand is growing exponentially.

The economic view of depletion anticipates that the real costs of finding and processing minerals will rise as producers are forced to turn to poorer deposits and that eventually this will force society to curtail its consumption of mineral products. Thus it is argued that the issue of scarcity is properly posed in terms of the costs of extracting certain resources in ever-increasing amounts and thereby the prices at which they will be available.

On the questions of depletion and scarcity, Harold Barnett and Chandler Morse took the lead in their seminal 1963 study entitled **Scarcity and Growth: The Economics of Natural Resource Availability**. Instead of relying on physical measures of the stocks of natural resources at any time, Barnett and Morse called for the use of scarcity indexes to signal the importance of growing limitations on these available stocks.

Their arguments centered on four factors that mitigated against increasing resource scarcity:

1. The occurrence of any particular natural resource is such that, as high grade sources are exhausted, lower grade sources are available in greater abundance
2. the increasing scarcity of a particular resource leads to increases in the rate of its price appreciation which induces greater substitution of other materials
3. these same price increases generate incentives for exploration for new deposits, and for recycling
4. technical change serves to continuously expand the prospects for using lower grade deposits and for substitution of new materials.[7]

Barnett and Morse drew a distinction between *Malthusian scarcity* (an absolute limit to natural resources, beyond which availability is nil) and *Ricardian scarcity* (unlimited resources in total but nonhomogeneous in quality). They concluded that Malthusian (or absolute) scarcity is not relevant and that only Ricardian (or relative) scarcity is of concern, and even that is being overcome. "Advances in fundamental science made it possible to take advantage of the uniformity of energy/matter — a uniformity that makes it feasible without preassignable limit, to escape the quantitative constraints imposed by the character of the earth's crust. . . . Science, by making the resource base more homogeneous, erases the restrictions once thought to reside in the lack of homogeneity. In a neo-Ricardian world, it seems, the particular resources with which one starts increasingly become a matter of indifference."[8] In sum, absolute scarcity is dismissed from further consideration, and even relative scarcity is deemed likely to be vanquished by the march of science. Stemming from this study, the dominant view of current orthodox economic theory has become that only relative scarcity matters.

In what proved to be another classic statement on natural resources, Harold Hotelling in a 1931 article entitled "The Economics of Exhaustible Resources" used the concept of present value maximization to explore what maximizes the present value of the stream of consumer benefits from the stock of natural resources.[9] Because the market encourages firms to maximize the present value of their profit stream, even with exhaustible resources, Hotelling wondered whether market forces would maximize the present value of consumer benefits. He found that under competitive conditions the market tends to lead toward present value maximization of consumer benefits.

It is important to note that Hotelling was working under the assumption that new resources can always be found or that technology will come up with suitable substitutes for the vital natural resources. In his worldview there was no such thing as absolute shortage or even its possibility. For the most part, the economics profession has followed Hotelling's line of analysis and has explicitly or implicitly assumed that for any rate of utilization of natural resources what is optimal for the consumption of the present generation will also be optimal for the consumption of future generations. As a result most economists have felt that no unique effort should be made in the conservation of natural resources.

In sum, economists maintain that the price mechanism will operate so as to increase the production of required resources — whether from newly discovered reserves, lower-grade or less economic reserves, the application of new technology to production, or the recycling of waste. This same mechanism will operate so as to bring about the substitution of lower-cost resources (even new ones), more efficient and more sparing use of scarce resources, and an increase in the durability of the goods produced from scarce resources.

Under free market conditions, a nonrenewable natural resource derives its market value from the prospect of its extraction and sale. If the free market is competitive, owners of nonrenewable resources could expect two things to happen: (1) the prices they could sell their resources for would increase as the supply diminished or the demand increased and (2) the value of their capital assests, that is, the nonrenewable resource still left in the ground, would also appreciate and at a rate equal to that of any equal-risk investment.

These two conditions define a truly exhaustible resource base. Implied here is the notion that both the stock (asset) and flow aspects of nonrenewable resources are interwoven. According to R. M. Solow, if these two aspects have been perfectly harmonized through the "operations of futures markets . . . the last ton [of any resource] produced will also be the last ton in the ground." In other words, "the resource will be exhausted at the instant it has priced itself out of the market.[10]

Standard economic theory also incorporates a perspective on market failures. Economists agree that the market is indeed flawed, but they go on to say that if the flaws were corrected, there would be no need for a national materials policy; the market would provide the right balance between depletion and conservation, disposal and durability, and so forth. If the market failures cannot be corrected, or if upon examination they turn out not to be failures at all but "distortions" to bend market allocations toward worthy and intended policy goals, then the market can still be used as a standard to measure by. According to this view:

> We estimate what the market would do in the absence of distortions, calculate the gaps by examining what the market is actually doing, and choose materials policy goals on the basis of closing these gaps. To follow this prescription is to act under the efficiency criterion. This criterion, which can be used as a basis for materials policy, says that material flows should be arranged as if they were operating in a perfect market.[11]

In this description of the conventional economic wisdom regarding natural resources, only the major principles have been highlighted, but the general thrust of the economists' perspective should be clear. Again, Barnett and Morse provide the most eloquent summary:

> Continual enlargement of the scope of substitutability — the result of man's technological ingenuity and organizational wisdom — offers those who are nimble a multitude of opportunities for escape. The fact of constraint does not disappear; it merely changes character. New constraints replace old, new scarcities generate new offsets.[12]

This conventional wisdom is fine in terms of the limited territory it covers and the restrictive assumptions imposed, but a more realistic and more holistic resource economics must be forged to meet the requirements of the future.

6

NATURAL RESOURCES: SHORTCOMINGS IN CONVENTIONAL THEORY

The primary fault of conventional economic theory lies with the restrictive assumptions on which it is based; these center on standard market assumptions, which often do not match up with real world realities. Some of the shortcomings become clear in taking a critical look at the market theory approach used in the Harold Barnett and Chandler Morse study — a study that forms the basis for the optimistic thinking among contemporary economists about the adequacy of natural resources.[1]

CRITIQUE OF THE BARNETT-MORSE STUDY

The most serious shortcoming in the study involves its definition of *natural resources*. Like all resource economists, the authors defined natural resources as those commodities that exchange on primary commodity markets. Hence their analysis of resource adequacy was limited to only those resources with ownership vested in private parties. The services provided by the whole range of common property environmental resources, including important elements of the basic life-support system, were omitted. Thus their analytical framework fails to recognize that the relaxation of the private property resource constraints — one of their principal findings — may have been achieved at the expense of reductions in the stock of common property services.

Interestingly, Barnett and Morse, in concluding their analysis, identified environmental quality and deterioration in the quality of life in general as sources of concern but implicitly regarded them as "separable" from any scarcity of natural resources. Yet, once those concerns are accepted as potentially important components in any appraisal of the adequacy of natural resources, there is reason to question any analysis such as theirs that relies exclusively on outcomes of market processes to furnish the answers.

There have been many empirical updates of the Barnett-Morse work, including a 1979 analysis by Barnett.[2] The evidence presented by Barnett suggested that there does not appear to be a growing scarcity in the supply of primary commodities, thus upholding the conclusion of the original study.

The other update studies, however, which have considered all three of the scarcity measures — real unit costs, neoclassical average costs, and relative prices — offered mixed findings.[3] Those updates based on the real unit cost measure have generally supported the original conclusions. The evidence found using neoclassical cost estimates and relative prices, on the other hand, seems to cast doubt on the original findings. Based on such diversity, one must conclude that the verdict on the adequacy of natural resources is not "in."

V. Kerry Smith, whose exhaustive work on this issue in recent years formed the basis for the above critique, succinctly summarizes where the economic theory of natural resources currently stands:

1. Past confidence in the increased availability of natural resources over time must be questioned. The theory of scarcity measures, empirical analyses, and character of the physical constraints all contribute to reservations on past conclusions.

2. Economic models concerned with the implications of a narrowing in the resource base, and their optimistic conclusions, should be reconsidered in light of the potential importance of open access environmental resources for such judgements.

3. Our empirical knowledge of the role of narrowly defined natural resources in exisiting technologies, and the change in these technologies over time, is quite primitive. However, what we do know seems to be at variance with several prominent economists' interpretations of the "facts". . . .

4. The treatment of engineering (i.e., production related) and physical constraints to economic activities may well require more detailed knowledge of these constraints than previously assumed. Economic models have thus far adopted convenient abstractions in representing those processes or factors limiting the scope for economic behavior.

Their assumptions have been called increasingly into question in resource and environmental economics. These questions suggest that many complex, resource-related problems may require a new, more specific, and inherently multidisciplinary approach.[4]

FALLACY OF PREDICTABILITY

Standard market theory is based on a set of predictability assumptions (the rationality of market participants, certainty regarding the future, and persistence of free markets) that stretch the bounds of credibility too far.

As the term has been traditionally used in economic analysis, *rationality* implies a degree of foresight about future gains and costs and an ability to weigh them against each other which are just not possessed by the economic actor. Belatedly, we are recognizing that in a world of uncertainty, and in an economic system that is inherently unstable, human economic behavior is much more irrational and erratic than that assumed in a theoretical world of equilibrium. Thus it will never be possible to make precise economic predictions regarding matters that depend so fundamentally on this very behavior.

There is also much uncertainty about future scarcities. In extractive industries such as mining, both future demand and future supply of a particular mineral resource are subject to major uncertainties. Supply is influenced by the success of further exploration and by developments in mining technology. Demand depends on future economic growth, possible substitutions, and changes in demographic and consumption patterns. Even if future shortages appear likely, their timing and magnitude are subject to considerable uncertainty.

Because of such uncertainty about both market actors and scarcity, futures markets for resources are not well established. This is a serious problem because a full set of future markets must exist for the market system to optimally allocate resources use over time as well as at a given time. Therefore, it should be possible today to make contracts about deliveries of goods and services in the future. The absence of future markets, according to resource economist Allen Kneese, "creates a systematic incentive to produce too much of a nonrenewable resource in the present at the expense of production in the future."[5] This, Kneese argues, is perhaps the most fundamental rationale for levying severance taxes and undertaking other nonenvironmentally based conservation measures with respect to extractive industries.

To the extent future markets for resources do exist, they are fraught with imperfections, not the least of which is inadequate information. Neither companies nor governments like to let their potential competitors know exactly what their reserves of nonrenewable resources are. Frequently they do not know themselves. Without such information, however, futures markets cannot function effectively. It is difficult to discount stocks at appropriate rates if these stocks are not known in the first instance. In addition, even if futures markets were well established, they would still be subject to a variety of surprises and shocks. There are surprises resulting from new technological applications for certain resources and from political events as well. The success of the OPEC cartel in jacking up — and subsequently maintaining — world oil prices at an "artificially" high level is the most obvious illustration.

Thus it appears reasonable to postulate that the risks associated with nonrenewable resources increase as one moves further into the future. A firm that wants to reduce risk will emphasize the more predictable near future. In the context of mining, this would result in a shift of extraction from the future to the present, thus reducing conservation. Then, assuming that other things remained equal, the severity of any future shortage or crisis would likely increase.

Economists have assumed that free markets will persist in the allocation of nonrenewable resources and that private hoarding and speculation are feasible means of conservation, withdrawing potentially scarce resources from current consumption. However, history demonstrates that whenever communities have been concerned with conserving resources (forests, fish, game, or a healthy environment), they had to introduce quantitative restrictions. When major scarcities of important goods or materials have developed, the almost universal reaction of societies has been to abandon the free market system in favor of some form of rationing. Examples of this type of social behavior are plentiful: food during a famine or in war; water during a drought; and in recent times, gasoline during an embargo.

While the assumption is that free markets will persist, many economic decisions are essentially "planned" corporate or governmental decisions (Galbraith's "planning system") rather than "market" decisions. And if nonrenewable resources are controlled in substantial measure by multinational corporations and by governments, that are operating in a "planning" system rather than in any pure market system, what happens when there are major institutional or behavioral changes on the part of the corporations and the governments involved? There can be enormous increases in prices due solely to the power of the controllers of the market to set prices, with these increases extending beyond those that are brought about by discontinuities in the market, particularly those on the supply side.

Thus institutional and behavioral changes can force adjustments that are far from smooth, adjustments beyond those anticipated by any market model — a model that by its very nature does not incorporate institutional and behavioral changes of this order. The importance of this problem can be seen in the special case of the petroleum price increases that began in early 1974. Few economists foresaw the formation of OPEC and what flowed from it.

FALSE ASSUMPTION OF MARKET EFFICIENCY

Three main factors cause markets to operate inefficiently: (1) government-induced distortions in the marketplace, (2) the market system's inability to include environmental and disposal costs in product prices, and (3) monopoly pricing power.

The prime source of government-induced distortions is the federal tax system. For instance, federal income taxes on the extractive sector have historically not been as heavy as on other sectors of the U.S. economy. This can be attributed to deliberate government efforts, dating back several decades, to encourage domestic resource development. These tax advantages have had two principal effects. Not only has extraction proceeded at a faster rate than it would have without differential tax treatment, but our primary materials industries have also, to some degree, developed at the expense of secondary materials industries. These policies have also tended to stimulate U.S. exports and inhibit imports. For 40 years economists have argued that the extractive sector is taxed too lightly relative to other sectors, leading to too much extraction, too much material and energy throughput, too much solid waste, and not enough recycling. Now it is gradually becoming apparent that the previous bias in the tax system has been an important cause of the solid waste problem.

A similarly biased intervention has occurred in railroad freight rates, regulated by the Interstate Commerce Commission (ICC). The cost of transporting a raw material is a large fraction of its price, and thus differences in transportation costs will be largely reflected in product prices. There is some evidence that transportation rates, particularly railroad freight rates, are not related to the actual cost of shipment and that scrap materials headed for recycling pay higher rates than virgin materials. In fact, it appears that some virgin materials pay less than the marginal cost of shipment.

Another failure of the market — to incorporate environmental costs and collection and disposal costs of waste and pollution into the prices of finished products — has long been suspected of leading to a higher rate of materials consumption than would otherwise be the case. Although many environmental costs have recently been "internalized" by industries' installation of pollution control equipment, substantial unincorporated environmental costs still exist. In the past, local governments have paid the cost of municipal waste disposal, just as society as a whole has paid the costs of breathing polluted air. The market system fails to incorporate these disposal costs in a product's price. Because the product prices do not reflect these social costs, they do not properly affect consumer decisions.

Another reason for market inefficiency is the concentration of resource ownership in the hands of private, public, or semipublic monopolies. Although industries processing virgin materials (primary industries) are not pure monopolies, they are typically dominated by a few large firms that show some evidence of the power (and will) to influence prices. In addition, the unstable relationships that exist between multinational corporations, which may derive their revenues largely from resource extraction and processing (such as the Arabian-American Oil Company [ARAMCO] in Saudi Arabia), and their host nations can further distort international market pricing.

OVEREMPHASIS ON THE INDIVIDUAL

The market model rests squarely on the idea that natural resources and the means of producing marketable goods from them are owned by individuals and that individuals purchase the goods. Thus human existence is assumed to be basically individual in character, with the relationships between individuals (so far as scarce material goods are concerned) reduced to economic transactions.

Separating in theory what are actually indissoluble links between people and between people and nature means that the inevitable conflict between individual ownership and common ownership is not accounted for. Air, fresh water, the oceans, and certain parts of the land (such as national parks and forests) are examples of "common property resources" that are being pressured by individual ownership abstracted from its ties with humanity or nature. This problem is compounded by the difficulty in communicating, harmonizing, and mobilizing the opinions of a large group of people, in contrast with the efficiency and speed with which an individual assesses and acts in his or her own interests.

EXCLUSION OF PHYSICAL PRINCIPLES

The conventional economic models do not incorporate physical principles: the laws of thermodynamics, which would require the acceptance of the concept of absolute scarcity. This fact, combined with a growing global population and growing per capita consumption, guarantees there will be increasing constraints placed on economic activity by absolute scarcity.

While the price system handles relative scarcity admirably, by itself it is largely powerless against absolute scarcity because it is impossible to raise the relative prices of all resources in general. Any attempt to do so merely raises the absolute price level, and instead of substitution — since there is no substitute for resources in general — we merely get inflation.

The "alternative" to dealing with absolute scarcity taken in orthodox economics has been to wish it out of existence. Malthus has been buried many times and Malthusian scarcity with him. But as Garrett Hardin has remarked, anyone who has to be reburied so often cannot be entirely dead.[6]

INADEQUATE ACCOUNTING FOR FUTURE GENERATIONS

Conservationists have long aimed to keep the resource base essentially intact from generation to generation. And when the resource base appears threatened, as it now does with respect to fossil fuels, preservation of this base becomes an important goal for society as a whole. Economists, on the other hand, have yet to include preservation of the resource base among macroeconomic goals requiring policy measures. They have preferred to rely on Adam Smith's "invisible hand" of the market to match new technology against depletion, much as before the Great Depression they counted on the invisible hand to eliminate unemployment.

Talbot Page has succinctly captured the inherent limitation of markets in this regard:

> Markets can be expected to allocate resources more or less efficiently relative to a given distribution of wealth or market power (a hypothetical ideal market would actually achieve efficiency). But markets cannot be expected to solve the problem of what is a fair or equitable distribution of wealth, either among different people at a point in time (intratemporally) or among different generations (intertemporally).[7]

The issues of depletion and creation of long-lived wastes are fundamentally those of equitable distribution of burdens that must be shared across generations. As material flows are becoming enormously larger, lead times shorter, and the environmental and technological effects more pervasive, it is time to make preservation of the resource base and environment an explicit policy issue, as it has not been since around 1910 when the conservation movement was at its zenith.

Even at that time, most economists who began to explore the appropriate rate of utilization of natural resources did not think of them as unique factors of production warranting special treatment. Conservationists, on the other hand, claimed not only that natural resources were unique but that mankind had a moral duty to preserve them for future generations as nearly unimpaired as the nature of the case would allow. Aldo Leopold, a leading conservationist, contended: "A system of conservation based solely on economic self-interest is hopelessly lopsided. It tends to ignore, and thus eventually to eliminate, many elements in the land community that lack commercial (economic) value, but that are . . . essential to its healthy function. It assumes that the economic parts of the biotic clock will function without the uneconomic parts.[8]

A few economists did attempt an analysis of the economic implications of natural resource utilization; at the University of Wisconsin,

Richard T. Ely and Lewis C. Gray led the way, as they explored the relationship between economic theory and natural resources. Gray's remarkable pioneer study, "Economic Possibilities of Conservation," appeared in 1913. He showed more insight than many later economists when he stated that "the real heart of the conservation problem presents an issue which taxes the resources of economic theory to the utmost. This issue is the problem of adjusting the conflict between the interest of the present and the future."[9]

Having begun his study by distinguishing between renewable and nonrenewable resources, Gray investigated the criterion of *present value maximization*, which discounts all monetary benefits from a future stream of natural resources to their present value and then maximizes this present value. This criterion was used by almost all later economists to determine the optimal rate of utilization of nonrenewable resources. Gray concluded that such a criterion would not aid in achieving conservation. More than a half century later, Page also critiqued the present value criterion in comparison to the conservationist criterion:

> If we stretch our imaginations to allow representatives from the future to participate in an up-or-down vote between criteria, it is hard to think that the present value criterion would prevail without some modification. To an assembly of representatives drawn from all generations, this criterion would not look much more attractive than the scheme of vesting total ownership and management of the oceans' fisheries to one country this year, to another the next year, to another the following year would look to an assembly of present-day countries.[10]

The focus on present value, combined with an equally simplistic economic assumption that all effective wants (whether for luxuries or for basic necessities) are equally justified, can only lead to abuse not only of natural resources but of human resources as well. Since the present value maximization criterion sets the value of everything, including the discount rate, strictly from the known wants of the present generation, one can ignore the really difficult and important question of what to do about absolute biophysical shortages as well as the consequent normative problem of choosing between present luxuries and future vital needs.

In many ways Gray's pioneering efforts reached a level of sophistication and breadth of understanding in combining economic theory and conservation principles that was not to be reached again for many years. It would be decades before economists would realize that the present value maximization criterion would not guarantee the welfare of future generations. Gray instinctively grasped what Talbot Page and James Doilney have recently laboriously proved: that present value maximization analysis is one thing and conservation is another thing and that both standards have to be considered when making societal decisions.[11]

At the heart of both the present value criterion and the conservationist criterion is the notion of discounting, which basically posits that resources and consumption in the present are more valuable than they will be in the future. Thus, any benefits from future use of resources or future consumption should be discounted. Inherent in the process of discounting is the fact that the free market mechanism will not allocate balanced quantities for each period until the resource is exhausted but will make more generous allocations in early periods, which get progressively smaller as time goes on. This occurs because discounting deemphasizes the future and does so at an accelerating rate as one moves through time. Furthermore, any conservation of resources for the future is likely to decrease with increasing discount rates. The higher the market discount rate, the steeper the price increase over time in a free market.

Whether free markets in this context will lead to an optimal conservation policy for society depends on whether market discount rates as applied by mine operators and investors coincide with the discount rate that society chooses to apply in trading off current versus future consumption. What the social discount rate should be is not an easy question, and the answer depends more on beliefs and philosophy than on scientific insights.

Actually, it should be asked, particularly in areas of strategic long-term importance, why should one discount at all, thereby favoring the current generation over future ones? Traditionally, one rationale that economists have given for discounting in this context is founded on the premise of continued economic growth. Assuming growth and consequent increases in living standards over time, why should the current generation sacrifice consumption for future generations who will be better off anyhow? Hence future benefits should be discounted, and heavier emphasis should be placed on increases in current consumption. This optimistic belief in continuous progress and growth is no longer universally accepted, and some current assessments of our economic future in the light of a growing world population and potentially decreasing resources are more cautious. If the living standards of the future were forecast to level off or decrease, future consumption would become progressively more important, and one could argue for zero or even negative discount rates on future benefits.

Whichever side of the argument one takes, the social discount rate, which should guide the management of exhaustible resources, need not coincide with the prevailing market rates. There are several reasons why society is likely to prefer a different depletion rate for its resources than are individuals. The most obvious one is that a society is expected to have a longer life span than an individual. Thus society would prefer to conserve a resource, while an individual, with no reason to be concerned for posterity (other than for existing children or grandchildren), would prefer to use it rapidly, reaping its benefits during his or her lifetime. Therefore, it would seem that if the rate of depletion is left to individuals, resources will be used more rapidly than is desirable for both human society and the whole community of life.

This discrepancy between the private and social discount rates is a primary example of the complications that plague the economists' concept of resource preservation. Theoretically, resource holders, seeing a limited stock of their resource and anticipating a future scarcity, would have the incentive of higher future prices to reserve some of their stock from the market. The problem is that resource preservation is just one factor among many market forces and may be submerged in complications and distortions of actual markets. These problems arise both at the company level and at the national government level.

At the company level, resource preservation depends upon estimating future potential profits and weighing them against the opportunity of present profits by means of a market interest rate or discount rate. It is possible that a large timber firm may look ahead 40 to 50 years and compare its present and future possibilities consistently with the efficiency criterion. But the firm's own timber managers may have a much shorter time horizon. A manager may realize that he must prove himself in just a few years and may want tangible results. He may discount the future at a much higher rate than the firm does, and his decisions may greatly determine the harvesting as well as the replanting rate.

Many depletable resources are located in developing countries and are exploited by multinational or foreign firms. Such firms may not weigh today's resource price against tomorrow's higher price. Tomorrow the firm may be nationalized, and the profits will go to someone else. Insecure tenure is not conducive to resource preservation.

As countries gain control of their resource bases, they may not act like competitive firms, but they may try to form cartels to control their markets. If they are successful, they may raise prices, slowing the rate of extraction. If only partially successful, they may destabilize the market, inducing large swings in price and material flows. On public land in the United States, mineral rights are acquired upon the discovery of the mineral in the same way that fish become owned upon their capture. This *rule of capture*, stemming from the 1872 mining law, tends to promote more mineral exploration and exploitation than the efficiency standard would call for, just as does the rule of capture in ocean fishing.

To conclude, our legacy to the future is not homogeneous. Intergenerational equity emerges as an important problem because there is no easy way to add up the costs and risks along with the benefits and no way to guarantee that the future is going to be better off than the present.

BENIGN NEGLECT OF GLOBAL INEQUITY

Economists have failed to recognize and cope with the emerging global issues in their full dimension; to reckon with the increasing insistence by peoples and nations on the importance of values other than purely economic ones; and to take into account the institutional changes that are creating major forces that operate outside of the market system.

It has fallen largely to noneconomists to identify and to seek to grapple with some of the grander issues. Sometimes these others have appeared to be cranks, but then, as Joan Robinson has observed, the cranks flourish "because the orthodox economists have neglected the great problems that everyone else feels to be urgent and menacing."[12]

The issues compelling consideration are common knowledge by now: a burgeoning population, particularly in those parts of the globe least able to support more people; limits on arable land and on the capital that can be applied to increase agricultural production; depletion of resources at rates that are already high and that would have to be increased to seemingly unattainable levels if the economic growth of Western nations were to be generalized around the globe; pollution and the degrading of the environment; and the slow pace in bringing technology to bear upon the resolution of these problems. The symptomatic problems that flow from the primary crises include famine in large areas of the globe, increasing tensions between the rich and the poor nations, and the menace of inflation in developed and developing nations alike.

Economists were forced belatedly to confront these issues in the 1970s by the call of developing nations for a New International Economic Order. The Third World demanded recognition that the root of the growing tensions between the developed and the developing countries was the enormous disparity between incomes and respective rates of growth and insisted that these be remedied.

The argument runs as follows: The advanced nations have exhausted their own supplies of many of the most important natural resources needed for an industrialized society and are entering into increased competition for the remaining supplies in the Third World countries. Continually increasing consumption by the industrial nations, which shortens supplies and raises prices, is now shutting off growth possibilities for the developing countries. In short, the industrial nations hold all of the cards in the present international division of labor, and it is now impossible for many developing countries to begin to catch up unless a dramatic transformation of the international economy takes place.

Clearly, the critical problems confronting the world involve institutional and behavioral issues as well as choices between economic and noneconomic values. Choices between market and nonmarket values must be made not only in the market system of economic theory but also in the planning system. For governments in this planning system, there may be another kind of market: the market of values, of traditions, of power, of fear, of bargaining — whatever ethical and behavioral forces enter into decision-making within this institutional framework. Economists will have to decide whether to content themselves with treating these factors as externalities — tracing through the economic consequences of these changes and choices once they are identified by others — or whether to seek to relate their discipline to take account of these fundamental forces.

The latter approach would entail incorporating the economic model into some larger model — a model that comprehends multiple values, multiple modes of analysis, and multiple methods of making decisions. The economists must become multidisciplinary in their approach: they must come to recognize with a greater humility than has sometimes been their wont the contribution that other disciplines can make to "economic" analysis.

7

FORGING A BIOECONOMICS

Marginal and incremental modifications to conventional theory, while helpful, are far from what is really needed: a thorough reconceptualization of economics that would in some sense stand prevailing theory on its head. Instead of largely ignoring the "land" factor (all physical matter and the environment) or treating its features as "externalities" to the ongoing workings of the economic process, economics should be reorganized around the fact that natural resources and the physical environment constitute the fundamental foundation upon which all economic activity is constructed. Such a new bioeconomics will be absolutely necessary as we enter an era in which our economic prosperity, the condition of our environment, and the quality of our lives will be greatly determined by how carefully we use our remaining nonrenewable resources and enhance and sustain our renewable resources.

It is quite ironic that the guiding economic philosophy of the day — supply-side economics — focuses solely on financial capital, completely neglecting the ultimate supply source: matter and energy. A genuine supply-side economics would focus on the fact that biological capital is equally as important as financial capital for achieving long-run sustainable growth.

Reshaping conventional theory in this fashion would be a return in large measure, to the roots of economics. Both the Physiocrats and the classical economists recognized the centrality of the resource base and made it an integral part of their analysis.

Even epistomology points to a reunion of *economics* and *ecology*, which share the same linguistic root *eco* — derived from the Greek word *oikos* for "house." Thus *economics* in its original sense meant "the management of one's own household" and was quite limited in scope. But from the beginning *ecology* has denoted a recognition of humanity's extended household: the worldwide community of living things in all the intricacies of their coherence and exchange. The economist Alfred Kahn can find no line between the two disciplines:

> Environmental values are economic values; it is in principle just as important, in the interest of economic efficiency and therefore economic welfare, to conserve our limited natural resources, to make wise and sparing use of our limited clean air, water, and living space, as it is to economize in the use of labor and capital; and using some of our limited economic resources to preserve or restore an acceptable environment is just as much a contribution to economic welfare as devoting them to travel, shelter, or national defense.[1]

An epistemological shift from the mechanistic economic paradigm that has prevailed during the past two centuries to a new holistic economic paradigm is involved in the development of bioeconomic theory and methodology.

THE MECHANISTIC ECONOMIC PARADIGM

Sir Isaac Newton's seventeenth century mechanistic physics is still applied in conventional economics. The endless number of laws, equations, and curves reflect the underlying view that it is possible to isolate economic components and their causal relationships. In the Newtonian perspective, the universe resembles the workings of a clock — a smooth, predictable place. Adam Smith lived in this clockwork world, passionately admiring Newton. It was natural that he viewed the economic system as a kind of self-correcting machine presided over by an invisible hand, with hidden but calculable forces and definite cause and effect relationships, which it was the task of the economist to discover, explain, and correct.

After Smith, in the first half of the nineteenth century, a debate raged in geological and biological circles between the *uniformitarians* and the *catastrophists*. The former argued that things were pretty much what they had always been and their preoccupation was with cyclical, not progressive, change. The catastrophists held to a new evolutionary creed that also incorporated a theory of sudden, violent, revolutionary change. This view generally triumphed in the end, backed by the success of Darwin's theory of the origin of species.

Newton's world all but ceased to exist for most sciences, both physical and social. There was no more clockwork universe — except in economics. Alfred Marshall and his **Principles of Economics**[2] dominated the late 1800s. The book's epigraph *natura non facit saltum* ("nature does nothing by sudden jumps") is pure uniformitarianism — Newton's "clockwork universe" married to the concept of equilibrium. Keynes, Marshall's star pupil, learned his lesson well. In Cambridge, England, the home of uniformitarianism for 50 years before Keynes was born, the concept came as easily to him as breathing.

Today in noncommunist countries, the mainstream of economics still follows the uniformitarianism of Newton, Adam Smith, Marshall, and Keynes. By and large contemporary economists have been happy to develop their discipline along the mechanistic tracks laid out by these forefathers, fighting any suggestion that economics might become anything other than what W. Stanley Jevons called "the mechanics of utility and self-interest."[3]

Jevons meant that the main objective of economics is determining the allocation of the given means toward the optimal satisfaction of the given ends. In this sense economics is a mechanical analogue, as is any system that involves a conservation principle (given means) and a maximization rule (optimal satisfaction). Thus the "myth," as Nicholas Georgescu-Roegen calls it,[4] is sustained that the economic process is a circular merry-go-round that cannot possibly affect the environment of matter and energy in any way.

As in mechanics the general rule for the economic process becomes complete reversibility — that any process can take place both forward and backward so that everything is just as it was in the beginning, with no trace left by the happening. Economics has drawn the reversible time concept directly from classical mechanics, which in turn derived it from the mathematics of Descartes (who, in assuming that time is cardinally measurable, also assumed time is reversible).

Having constructed its theory of equilibrium on a uniformitarian base, it is no wonder that economics has been essentially a "timeless" science. It operates in a world characterized by changing short-run equilibriums. Unfortunately, the world does not operate in that manner. In fact, rates and patterns of economic growth are being changed significantly by a series of underlying long-run forces. Such a fundamental evolutionary change from one economic world into the next simply cannot be captured by short-run equilibrium analysis.

Carl Madden succinctly conveyed the shortcomings of economic theory in this regard:

> Economic theory studies the allocation of resources among competing ends, assuming that tastes, technology and resources are given. In analyzing the relationships between revenues and costs, economists pay little or no regard to evolutionary processes, to the dissipation of energy, or to the depletion of resources. These aspects of the economic process are considered, if at all, as "externalities," that is, as costs or benefits which are "external" to the theory of the firm or market. Unwittingly, because of the Cartesian concept of time, economists have failed to realize that waste and pollution are not "external" to the economic process, that time in the real world of ongoing events is not reversible.[5]

The concepts of mechanics, uniformitarianism, and reversible time all stem from the first law of thermodynamics. Up until recent years the relationship of the economic process to the second law, the entropy law, was ignored. This was a critical mistake, for what Georgescu-Roegen calls "the irreducible opposition" between the analogues of mechanics and of modern thermodynamics stems from the entropy law, which recognizes that even the material universe is subject to an irreversible qualitative change, to an evolutionary process. Today it is widely acknowledged that any life process is governed not by the laws of mechanics but by the entropy law. This point, Georgescu-Roegen states, is most transparent (but also most widely unrecognized) in the case of the economic process:

> The economic process, like any other life process, is irreversible (and irrevocably so); hence, it cannot be explained in mechanical terms alone. It is thermodynamics, through the Entropy Law, that recognizes the qualitative distinction which economists should have made from the outset between the inputs of valuable resources (low entropy) and the final outputs of valueless waste (high entropy).[6]

A HOLISTIC ECONOMIC PARADIGM

A new economic paradigm would extend economic analysis with regard to scope of data, time, and space to encompass consideration of many noneconomic factors and trends to develop a long-run analysis capability and to incorporate the workings of the global economy and subnational economies.

A holistic view would assume that the distinction between what is economic and what is noneconomic tends to break down. Currently, economists often discuss the economy as though it were hermetically sealed off from the sociopolitical system and from physical resources and physical principles. Long-run "economic" growth is viewed primarily as economic in nature rather than as an irreversible process of cultural and social, as well as economic, change. Establishing the latter perspective is essential if we are to resolve the difficult problems confronting the country regarding energy, the environment, and natural resources, all of which involve economic, technical, and social aspects.

Through a holistic economic paradigm, the economic system would be viewed as a subsystem and assessed in an overall context that accounts for the interactions among the various subsystems. For example, the traditional postulate that the government should be allowed to decide upon the volume of aggregate demand to secure the full use of the overall capacity of the economy would be questioned by holistic economics since such a postulate may conflict with those that relate to the functioning of other subsystems. Higher aggregate demand, though leading to higher output and employment, may simultaneously lead to an increase in the depletion of energy and nonrenewable resources, aggravating the ecological imbalance. *Interrelatedness* in the industrial sector means that there is a direct link between (1) technology and capital accumulation and (2) the depletion of nonrenewable resources and the impairment of the ecological equilibrium.

The new paradigm would necessitate an interdisciplinary approach. Unfortunately, professional economists, in their quest for scientific purity and quantitative elegance, tend to avoid collaborative efforts with those in other disciplines. This tunnel vision is actually symptomatic of a broader problem of disciplinary overspecialization whereby food problems belong to agriculture, energy to engineering, employment and inflation to economics, and adaptation to psychologists and geneticists. Though each speciality can produce valuable insights, the sum of all these specialized utterances will not add up to coherent solutions because the problems are not independent and sequential but highly interrelated and simultaneous. Thus the whole must be examined, even if it means — as it inevitably will — foregoing full knowledge of all the parts. Stephen E. Harris has forcefully summarized the case.

> In no science are the forces, processes, and relationships more varied and complex than in political economy. Any catalog of the barest minimum of historical, technical, political, social, psychological, and biological detail which political economy must encompass would indicate the need for integrative and inductive reasoning of a high order. As for the economists themselves, they must be Renaissance thinkers, not narrow-minded scholastics.[7]

ELEMENTS OF BIOECONOMICS

Current theory — in which the physical principles and conditions must accommodate the autonomous nonphysical conditions — must be upended so that physical parameters such as net energy, physical resource availability, a complex ecosystem, and the laws of thermodynamics take priority. It must be asked how the nonphysical variables (such as technology, capital, preferences, and the distribution of wealth and income) can be brought into a sustaining equilibrium with the complex biophysical system.

Alfred Marshall, one of the giants of economic thought, would have felt at home with this approach because he asserted that as economics became a mature science, biological analogies were to be preferred to mechanical analogies. Perhaps his most forceful statement was that "the Mecca of the economist lies in economic biology rather than in economic dynamics."[8] Indeed, most of the leading economic thinkers, beginning with Adam Smith and continuing through Malthus and Marx to Keynes, acknowledged in their writings the significance of biological-economic analogies.

Biological Capital

Bioeconomics must explore the relationship between conventional capital (buildings, equipment, and so forth) and biological capital (the *ecosphere*). The course of environmental deterioration indicates that as conventional capital has accumulated since 1946, the value of biological capital has declined. Environmental degradation therefore represents a crucial, potentially fatal, hidden factor in the operation of the economic system. Thus the effect of the operation of the economic system on the value of its biological capital needs to be taken into account to obtain a true estimate of the overall wealth-producing capability of the system.

Going a step further, biological capital essentially consists of solar-energy income and fossil fuel–minerals capital. This basic distinction, so common in most economic and business affairs, has been lost in the area where it really matters: the irreplaceable natural capital that man has not made but simply found, without which he can do nothing.

To understand the importance of this distinction consider whether a business leader would consider a firm to have solved its problems of production and to have achieved viability if that firm were rapidly consuming its capital. The answer is obvious, yet this vital fact has been overlooked when it comes to the economy of planet earth. Why? Most fundamentally, it is because we are estranged from reality and inclined to treat as valueless everything that we have not made ourselves. In the words of Bertrand de Jouvenel:

> He [Western man] tends to count nothing as an expenditure, other than human effort; he does not seem to mind how much mineral matter he wastes and, far worse, how much living matter he destroys. He does not seem to realise at all that human life is a dependent part of an ecosystem of many different forms of life. As the world is ruled from towns where men are cut off from any form of life other than human, the feeling of belonging to an ecosystem is not revived. This results in a harsh and improvident treatment of things upon which we ultimately depend, such as water and trees.[9]

A New Perspective On Value

When it comes to natural resources and ecosystems, there is considerable ambiguity surrounding the concept and use of the word *value* among economists and ecologists. The basic difficulty lies in the fact that there are three distinct values associated with any given natural resource and ecosystem.[10] Economists generally focus on one or two, while ecologists will often go beyond to the third intangible value, thus leaving economists behind. It is this third type of value that bioeconomists must encompass. The basic differences among the three types can be best understood by examining the various "values" of tropical forests.

The most clearly understood value is *market value*, which is clearly defined as *market price*. This price reflects "true" value (in an economic sense) when the assumptions of the market model — that is, uninhibited competition in a free enterprise system — are met in the marketplace.

The market value items of tropical forests are legion. Individuals increase their wealth at a local level through trade of food, fiber, and wood on the marketplace. Marketable products are primarily (1) lumber in the form of logs, plywood, veneer, and fiber used for paper and (2) freely harvested crops. Market value is also derived through conversion to agriculture in the forms of pasture, row crops, and tree plantations. Finally, food products (fruits, nuts, and oils), chemicals (resin and oils), and pharmaceuticals (caffine and quinine) are extracted from tropical plants and marketed.

The second value type is nonmarket value of public goods and services that are attributable or assignable. Here, items are assigned price or value through a political mechanism because a society believes that marketplace mechanisms inadequately assign values to the items. Examples of such items for tropical forests are maintenance of global air quality, aesthetic and recreational benefits, and the preservation of genetic stocks.

These first two values that economists deal with are established by institutional mechanisms, mainly the market and the political system. The final value type items, intangible or nonassignable non-market goods and services, are difficult to evaluate because they have not been incorporated into any agreement system. They are principally ecological benefits that private market economics cannot price. Although these items are designated as nonattributable, it would be the intent of bioeconomics to eventually have values assigned to them. Examples of such items for tropical forests are the intrinsic value of species, culture, and ecosystems; a natural laboratory for the study of natural selection, nutrient cycling, and so on; a habitat for native people; the natural life-support sytems that provide free service; the maintenance of the global carbon balance and atmospheric stability; the inherent values of natural systems.

Certainly a number of currently nonassignable value items will continue to defy the assignment of monetary values and thus simply cannot be placed in an economic valuation system. However, since they are items of intrinsic worth, they should be enumerated and considered in any decision-making process regarding alteration of natural resources.

Entropy

The potentially most fundamental change would be the full integration of the entropy law, the second law of thermodynamics, into economics. This law is the true taproot of economic scarcity. The law basically posits that matter and energy can only be changed in one direction, from usable to unusable, from ordered to disordered, from available to unavailable. As related to economics, the law implies that all production processes transform valuable natural resources (low entropy or freely available matter-energy) into commodities and eventually waste (high entropy or bound and unavailable matter-energy).

The very origin of the concept of thermodynamics was permeated with its relationship to economics. Sadi Carnot (1837-1894), in a memoir on the efficiency of steam engines, explored how to determine the conditions under which one could obtain the highest output of mechanical work from a given input of free heat. Every subsequent development in thermodynamics has added new proof of the bond between the economic process and thermodynamic principles. Georgescu-Roegen goes so far as to say that thermodynamics, as Carnot unwittingly set it going, is largely a physics of economic value.[11]

Despite this close relationship, it is fair to say that none of the physical content of thermodynamics has had any direct impact on economics of resource use. To understand what is meant by *direct impact*, we must consider what thermodynamics tells us: it is a science that specifies limits on the possible, in terms of idealized processes and what they can achieve. As Herman Daly expressed it: "The effect of the Entropy Law is as immediate and concrete as the facts that you can't burn the same tank of gasoline twice, that organisms cannot live in a medium of their own waste products, and that efficiencies cannot reach, much less exceed, 100%."[12]

Hence as a tool for economics, thermodynamics is a source of information about constraints. Thermodynamics is not and should not be thought of as a source of information about economic optimality; this is a condition that reflects the consequences of human preference. We must be extremely careful to avoid the simplistic but beguiling notion that thermodynamic extrema can be identified with economic optima. This identification, tantamount to an energy theory of value, could easily lead us to authoritarian technocracy.

In brief, in ignoring entropy economists have failed to realize that in a productive process entropy is just as inherent as productivity; that the product of the economic process is bound energy or waste and that, other things being the same, waste increases in greater proportion than the intensity of economic activity.

Georgescu-Roegen has examined the distinctions between the economic entropic process and the physical entropic process.[13] First, the entropic process of the material environment is automatic in the sense that it goes on by itself. The economic process, on the contrary, is dependent on the activity of human individuals who sort and direct environmental low entropy according to some definite rules, although these rules may vary with time and place. Thus, while in the material environment there is only shuffling, in the economic process there is also a sorting activity. Second, the economic process is actually more efficient than automatic shuffling in producing higher entropy, that is, waste. What, then, could be the raison d'être of such a process? The answer is that the true "output" of the economic process is not a physical outflow of waste but the enjoyment of life. According to Georgescu-Roegen:

> We cannot arrive at a completely intelligble description of the economic process as long as we limit ourselves to purely physical concepts. Without the concepts of purposive activity and enjoyment of life we cannot be in the economic world. And neither of these concepts corresponds to an attribute of elementary matter or is expressible in terms of physical variables.[14]

In Georgescu-Roegen's discussion of usefulness and economic value, he begins with the brute fact that low entropy is a necessary condition for a thing to be useful. But usefulness by itself is not accepted as a sufficient cause of economic value even by the discriminating economists who do not confuse economic value with price. To Georgescu-Roegen it is again thermodynamics that explains why the things that are useful also have an economic value (not to be confused with price). He uses land as an example because although it cannot be consumed, it derives its economic value from two sources: first, it is the only net with which we can catch the most vital form of low entropy; and second, the size of the net is immutable. He finds that "other things are scarce in a sense that does not apply to land, because, first, the amount of low entropy within our environment (at least) decreases continuously and irrevocably, and second, a given amount of low entropy can be used by us only once."[15]

This is why he stresses that the real payoffs are in durability, which reduces the flow of production-consumption-waste-recycling to the lowest level achievable. To accomplish this a critical applied part of bioeconomics would be the development of simulations of entire economic processes from extraction to refining, to manufacture, to consumption, to waste, to recycling in order to assess their relative efficiencies in resource utilization and concomitant pollution and depletion rates.

The concept of scarcity lies at the heart of the law of entropy — itself the taproot of economic scarcity. We must not overlook, however, the fact that scarcity also stems from the finitude of resources. It would therefore be a mistake for an economist to argue — as Robert Solow does — that we must not take into account this finitude because it cannot "lead to any very interesting conclusions."[16]

Once again considering land, even though it is not depletable, it has scarcity value because it limits the yearly flow of captured solar radiation. The scarcity of terrestrial resources, however, is far more severe since their stock is both finite and irrevocably exhaustible. Georgescu-Roegen feels the ultimate reason for the paramount importance of this scarcity is clear: "Ever since the human species transgressed the purely biological mode of adaptation, mankind has relied on detachable (exosomatic) organs — arrows, knives, clothes, carts, etc. — whose production requires terrestrial resources. Moreover, some of these detachable organs are now as crucial for the human's survival as the endosomatic ones."[17]

Low entropy exists in two forms — a terrestrial stock and a solar flow — both of which are limited but yet quite different in degree of scarcity. The terrestrial stock, both energy and material, consists of those renewable on a human time scale and those renewable only over geologic time and that, for human purposes, must be treated as nonrenewable. Terrestrial nonrenewables are limited in total amount available. Terrestrial renewables are also limited in total amount available and, if exploited to exhaustion, become just like nonrenewables. In terms of low entropy the stock of mineral resources is only a very small fraction of the solar energy received by the globe within a single year. More precisely, the highest estimate of terrestrial energy resources does not exceed the amount of free energy received from the sun within four days! In addition, the flow of the sun's radiation will continue with the same intensity (practically) for a long time to come.

So it is the meager stock of the earth's resources that constitutes the crucial scarcity. Resources can be substituted and new resources can be developed; but all of this occurs within the strictly limited total of low-entropy sources, and no rearrangement or substitution within the limited total will increase the total. Substitution will increase the efficiency with which the total terrestrial stock is used but not the size of the total stock. Thus the deus ex machina of economics — substitution — also has its limits, for substitution is always of one source of low entropy for another, and there is no substitute for low entropy itself.

Herman Daly believes that the failure to pay attention to ultimate means — the usable "stuff" of the universe, that is, low entropy — has led to an enormous and elementary economic mistake: becoming dependent on the scarce sources rather than on the abundant sources.[18] The seductive advantage of terrestrial stocks is that they can be used at a rate of man's own choosing (that is, rapidly), while the rate of solar flow is limited and interrupted by seasonal and diurnal variations. Rapid growth is easier when fueled with terrestrial stocks because these stocks can, for a while at least, be depleted as rapidly as we wish. The other side of the coin of rapid depletion of terrestrial stocks is abundant short-run supplies, low prices, and lavish use.

The rapid growth of the last 200 years has occurred because man broke the budget constraint of living on solar income and began to live on geological capital. Eventually, the geological capital will, for all practical purposes, run out. But to Daly, an even greater problem exists:

> The entire evolution of the biosphere has occurred around a fixed point — the constant solar-energy budget. Modern man is the only species to have broken the solar-income budget constraint, and this has thrown him out of ecological equilibrium with the rest of the biosphere. Natural cycles have become overloaded, and new materials have been produced for which no

natural cycles exist. Not only is geological capital being depleted but the basic life-support services of nature are impaired in their functioning by too-large a throughput from the human sector.[19]

At this point in the argument, it must be acknowledged that the real issue is more than economic, shading into the ethical: Should we undertake the discipline of living on income, or should we just consume capital while it lasts? The choice between oil and gas (both fossil fuels), or the choice between photovoltaic and biomass conversion (both solar), is the proper domain of economic calculation. But the choice between solar and fossil fuels is of a different order. Daly calls the decision more "heroic" or ethical in nature than "economic" in the usual sense of *marginal calculation.*

Why do we insist on ignoring the ethical character of so many major economic decisions? Why this compulsion to substitute mechanical calculation for responsible value judgment? Daly answers:

> Perhaps it's because our mechanistic paradigm has reduced values and ethics to mere matters of personal taste, about which it is useless to argue. Quality involves difficult judgments and imposes self-definition and responsibility. Quantity involves merely counting and arithmetical operations that give everyone the same answer and impose no responsibility.[20]

Georgescu-Roegen's view of these issues of quality, admittedly controversial, deserves serious consideration. He begins by noting that while the entropic process occurs at a gradual pace in nature, it is greatly accelerated by man in his quest for ever-more productive technologies and higher levels of consumption. Since the amount of matter-energy from which all useful materials must be derived is finite, the speed with which this endowment is used up will determine how long growth and, ultimately, life itself can be sustained on earth.

> It is the amount of terrestrial resources that determines the possible life span of the human species . . . And being finite, it sets an upper bound to the "amount of life" of the human species measured in man-years . . . The upshot is that, in the ultimate analysis, the economy of resources hinges mainly on demand.[21]

This premise leads Georgescu-Roegen to insist that living generations have a moral obligation to limit (and, indeed, to reduce) population and the rate of entropy to "minimize the regrets" of some future generation that must cope with a difficult and possibly violent adjustment as the requirements of our materials-intensive and polluting society outstrip the remaining beneficence of the planet. We have this obligation, he argues, whether the physical limits to growth are close at hand or far away. Even reversion to a steady state (that is, zero growth) will not save mankind indefinitely in this longest of runs, because even a steady state involves entropy increase. To him, curtailment of population to a level that could be fed by organic agriculture would provide the longest period of survival for our species. He notes that the world population explosion of the present era brings the adjustment period closer and threatens to make it painful.

The time has come for economists to acknowledge that although the books of the market system seem to balance and record economic progress, the books of nature, which render the real accounting for the human race, run increasing deficits. Market theory suffers from the inherent flaw that it ignores the cost of rising entropy. Market economics strives for economic efficiency. The new bioeconomists must also focus on entropic efficiency — the least amount of low-entropy use per unit of final consumption — which may ultimately prove to be more relevant to human welfare and development than economic efficiency.

CARRYING CAPACITY

All of the foregoing leads to the basic need to incorporate such biological concepts as *carrying capacity* and the *S-shaped growth curve* into economic theory and analyses. There is a strong intellectual basis for doing so in that carrying capacity expresses the function that Adam Smith ascribed to the invisible hand.

Smith's economy was largely based on nature's economy, and, based on his understanding of how the natural ecosystem functioned, he was correct. He saw a nature that was prodigious in her diversity and profligate in her abundance and thus had no way of knowing that the diversity and abundance of the ecosystem resources could be taxed beyond the capacity of the ecosystem to maintain itself. This, of course, violates the concept of carrying capacity, which is based on the recognition that all ecosystems are finite and have limits beyond which they cannot be maintained.

Hence in developing and applying bioeconomics, economists will need to take into account not only the diminishing returns of economics but also the negative returns associated with overexploiting nature. For example, a global economy expanding at 4 percent a year will eventually be forced to rely upon resources of diminishing quality. Technological advances may for a time more than offset declines in resource quality, but at some point even the most ingenious attempts to compensate for nature will no longer be adequate.

The fact that Adam Smith's economic philosophy incorporated the concept of unlimited growth is not surprising and indeed was the natural outgrowth of the period in which he lived. He was writing at a time when England was making the major shift from a renewable resource society to a nonrenewable resource society.

In a renewable resource society, the conditions of using natural resources efficiently sets up a negative feedback loop governing growth because renewable energy and materials are only available to the extent that the regenerative processes that provide them are not destroyed. Hence the worldview of such a society is one of limits that parallel the ubiquitous limits of the natural order. The use of nonrenewable resources truncates the age-old negative feedback loop that moderates growth, and hence nonrenewable resource societies developed a worldview of limitless expansion.

Resource management practices differed dramatically in each type of society. In the renewables society the centerpiece was conservation, while in the nonrenewable society it was rapid growth constrained only by technology and consumption.

Broadly viewed, in a renewables society there was a physical view of society that focused on processes by which resources are fashioned into production units, villages or cities, communication and transportation systems — all the elements that take a long time and that change very slowly. In the nonrenewable era, an economic view of society prevailed that focused on short-term market operations that are driven by money.

Once again we are facing a period of great transition, returning to a much greater reliance on renewable resources. In such a period, when economics can no longer assume that resources are given or infinite, economic policy alternatives must be evaluated as they relate to long-run ecological balance, not just to traditional economic variables such as investment, prices, employment, and income. Such a milestone in economic thought would lead to changes in the very definitions of *output, income, wealth, productivity, cost,* and *profit.*

Most important, the shift in the underlying energy resources base will lead, as it always has, to a shift in social structure. This is inevitable because societies organize around their energy systems in such a way that the characteristics of the energy system radiate out to influence every nook and cranny of society. Thus the final three chapters, which examine what the actual policies and practices could or should be in forging the transition to a renewable resources economy, are not solely economic and/or technological. They are fundamentally concerned with oncoming changes in the values, customs, knowledge, and institutions of the American people.

III
The Practice

8

CONSERVATION-MINDED SOCIETY

We need to become a conservation-minded society if we are to maintain and rejuvenate our soils, fisheries, forestlands, and recreational resources through a judicious blend of investments. We must also become a conservation-minded society if we are to change our water, energy, and resource policies to restore the wealth and vitality of our resource base as a rich inheritance for future generations.

What, specifically, is *conservation*? President William Howard Taft once said, "There are a great number of people in favor of conservation no matter what it means." Many popular definitions of *resource conservation* have been given. Gifford Pinchot, the well-known early conservationist, was among the most prolific creators of definitions. Two prime examples are: "Conservation is the use of natural resources for the greatest good of the greatest number for the longest time" and "Conservation implies both the development and protection of resources, the one as much as the other."[1] Unfortunately, like most definitions, Pinchot's were internally inconsistent and very vague and this vagueness meant they were of little use to policy.

At the most basic level, *resource conservation* simply means consuming less virgin natural resources than we otherwise would. More broadly, *conservation* can be defined as the process of prolonging the useful life of resources, either by preserving or by using and recycling.

Conservation can occur at any or all stages in the life cycle of a material: less total extraction; more complete use of what is extracted (less waste); longer-lived products and multiple use of materials before disposal (more reuse, recycling, or conversion into energy); and in the case of renewable resources such as timber, more replanting and improved husbandry of the land.

Immediately, the concept of conservation to many people conjures up images of a return to pioneer life-styles and tremendous sacrifice. While some degree of sacrifice will probably be involved, it need not be great. Adherence to fundamental conserving principles can provide the basis for both continued gains in standards of living and attainment of the quality-of-life objectives increasingly sought by Americans.

A wide variety of choices either to consume or to conserve material resources are made every day:

- Individuals purchase and use an enormous array of products in many types of packaging. When they have finished using them, a small fraction is set aside for reuse or recycling; most is simply discarded as waste. Although individuals do have opportunities to change this pattern—through selective buying, reuse, and increased recycling—these opportunities are generally limited and there is little incentive to take advantage of them.

- Private companies decide what combinations and quantities of materials will go into their products and packaging and what to do with the scrap materials left over from the manufacturing process. Relative price and customer preferences generally dictate these choices.

- Local government officials decide what to do with municipal solid waste: whether materials and energy will be recovered from it and how residents of their community will pay the bill for waste management. Local tax and land use policies are often major determinants in these choices.

- Federal officials make decisions about taxes, trade policies, subsidies, and regulations which broadly affect the choices by individuals, private companies, and local government officials to produce, consume, recycle, and dispose of materials. The full range of national goals and objectives enter into these decisions, and tradeoffs must be made among conflicting objectives.[2]

We cannot avoid choices to consume or conserve resources at any decision-making level; "business as usual" itself involves choices.

Whether by design, often without regard for the full costs to the public, most choices have been to use more (and reclaim fewer) resources. Such choices may have served us well when our "Land of Plenty" was first developed, but in this era of increasingly serious resource constraints, they are no longer wise.

Nowhere is this better seen than in the energy arena. In the era of cheap and abundant energy (up to 1973), we could design our factories, heavy machinery, cars, appliances, and even our agricultural system and our cities with little if any thought to their energy demands. In the last ten years all of this has had to be turned upside down. We, operating through marvelously efficient and powerful market forces, have come a long way already in energy conservation. Yet we still have a long way to go to achieve the measures described by Willis Harman that lead toward an energy-frugal society:

1. Redesign agriculture's dependence on fossil fuel derivatives by using less mechanized equipment and less fertilizer; disperse farming to place products closer to consumers; reduce processing and energy-wasteful packaging of food.
2. Reduce industrial consumption of energy by producing more durable, repairable goods (eliminating planned obsolescence), by designing for materials recycling, by altering production processes so that waste heat and materials from one process become inputs into another; change the product mix of the economy to include less energy-consumptive materials and services; disperse manufacturing to produce goods closer to raw material sources and to users; emphasize craftmanship and aesthetic quality rather than quantity of goods; emphasize sophisticated but frugal technology (e.g., the integrated-circuit hand calculator).
3. Reduce personal energy requirements by dispersing population to reduce transportation needs from residence to place of work, by increasing dependence on communication instead of transportation (utilizing electronic communications and miniaturized information processing systems), by curbing consumption of energy-intensive goods and services, and by stimulating community-based recreation instead of long-distance travel.
4. Redesign communities to be more self-sufficient and better suited to the environment and ecology, while using sophisticated technology to support highly civilized living conditions, not primitive privation (e.g., by using local solar heating, by employing intensive organic agricultural methods for food production, by reducing requirements for transportation).[3]

The beauty of such an energy policy is that it simultaneously optimizes social, economic and environmental goals. Chief among the advantages of a combined policy of conservation and renewables are:

- It slows down the required rate of capital formation for conventional energy source development, which is antiinflationary, and allows for greater flexibility and balance in the allocation of capital to social, economic, and environmental goals;
- It is labor- rather than energy- and capital-intensive, and this is an excellent generator of jobs; and
- In addition to creating jobs, it creates a broader distribution of jobs by type and location.

Clearly, movement toward an energy-frugal society and a conservation-minded society in general will require drastic changes in personal values, consumption habits, industrial structure, social institutions and national goals. It is to these we now turn.

CHANGE IN PERSONAL VALUES

At the most fundamental level, whether the United States becomes a conservation-oriented society depends primarily on the values, attitudes, and priorities adopted by the people. Since most problems that beset our society encroach gradually and are caused by the day-to-day behavior of individuals, they can be ultimately resolved only by a change in that behavior.

It has been argued that during the next two decades Americans will be forced to learn to live with new scarcities and to acquire habits of personal and social thrift. Daniel Yankelovich and Bernard Lefkowitz, however, found from their survey of public opinion polls taken over the period 1976–80 that the American public may already be at the leading edge of the conservation ethic.[4] Though people are not ready to give up those things they consider essential to their well-being and freedom (their cars, central heating, washing machines), they are prepared to make modest cutbacks in the use of energy, to keep their cars longer, to reduce consumption of meat and clothing, and to reduce their use of items that cannot be recycled if these involve waste. Based on such data, Yankelovich and Lefkowitz believe there is movement toward a more conserving society that is being accelerated by three significant psychosocial developments: a heightened emphasis on economic security, lowered economic expectations, and new values. They therefore conclude that the future will bring a more conserving society with a greater balance than now exists between consumption-oriented values and nonmaterialistic values.

A very recent investigation of how Americans are reacting to the dual objectives of economic progress and environmental protection is most revealing.[5] Drawing upon interviews with the general public, senior executives of large and small corporations, and members of major environmental groups, the study clearly shows that the public's continued desire for economic growth is moderated by strong quality-of-life considerations:

- 77% assert that protecting nature should be a high priority
- 76% agree that the earth is like a spaceship with only limited room and resources
- 49% said we must accept a slower rate of economic growth in order to protect the environment
- 72% agree with the statement "I believe American beliefs and values have been a basic cause of our environmental problems"
- 68% think more stress should be put on teaching people to live with basic essentials rather than on reaching a higher standard of living.

Certainly, American citizens retain an enduring commitment to revitalizing the economy, along with a sharp awareness that they live in a world of fragile natural balances that must be protected.

CORPORATIONS AS CRITICAL FRONT-LINE ACTORS

Corporations should be critical front-line actors in shaping a conservation-minded society, with much of their conserving activity activated by the dictates of market forces. This would lead to a rather significant change in corporate philosophy and mode of operation. Corporations would have to place greater emphasis on the development of production methods, technologies, and products that extend the life of renewable resources; maximize the sustainable yield of renewable resources; reduce energy and resource use per unit of output; eliminate or cut down on the creation of waste; allow for recycling; provide for greater longevity and durability; and ensure that they do not overburden the "public service" functions (such as waste assimilation) rendered by the natural environment.

To accomplish all this, corporations would need to launch a design revolution to improve the performance (basically, energy efficiency) and durability of consumer goods. Products designed to be durable, to use less materials, to be easily repaired, to pollute less, and to have lower operating costs would suddenly be recognized for their value — their life-cycle costs would be lower than competing, less efficient brands. Design possibilities include using corrosion-resistant materials, replacing rubber belts with gears, sealing sensitive parts, using modular construction for easy repair, and updating and developing synergetic (doing more with less) innovations. A related design challenge is to make a product easily recyclable by having parts that are readily separable.

Corporations may well adopt in the 1980s an environmentally oriented mode of industrial project planning, one in which inputs and means related to environmental concerns, values, processes, conditions, and interrelationships are continuously and carefully taken into account during planning. Since the object of environmentally oriented planning is the avoidance, or at least the minimization, of adverse environmental consequences, the range of areas for possible actions includes plant locations, input mixes, construction methods, scales of activity, process technologies, transport systems, and output patterns.

Environmentally sound planning could yield economic, political, and technical payoffs such as the avoidance of delays, smoother relations with the public and government agencies, better protection against spurious allegations, and the development of expertise that could be sold to other companies. Thus, environmental, energy, and economic interests would tend to converge to put a premium upon greater and greater efficiency in the industrial process — a new efficiency that can, at one and the same time, cut costs, conserve energy, and curb pollution.

A NEW GOVERNMENT PERSPECTIVE

We have become great in a material sense because of the lavish use of our resources, and we have just reason to be proud of our growth. But the time has come to inquire seriously what will happen when our forests are gone, when the coal, the iron, the oil, and the gas are exhausted, when the soils shall have been still further impoverished and washed into the streams, polluting the rivers, denuding the fields, and obstructing navigation. These questions do not relate only to the next century or to the next generation. One distinguishing characteristic of really civilized men is foresight; we have to, as a nation, exercise foresight for this nation in the future.[6]

These presidential words were not spoken by a president in recent years but by Theodore Roosevelt in 1911 in his keynote remarks to a White House Conference on the Conservation of Natural Resources. Unfortunately, the nation has not heeded his advice. Indeed, many Americans are deeply disturbed because they perceive that the United States is walking backwards into the future. With no vision of what the United States could or should be like, the nation drifts into an uncertain future like a ship without a compass or even a clear destination.

Key federal decision makers not only fail in vision, but they continue to view trends as isolated phenomena even though it is the mode of interaction among the major forces and trends influencing long-term growth that is usually critical in determining their ultimate impact. Tackling problems on such a piecemeal basis leads to policy "solutions" that are too narrowly based and often produce results favorable in one area but counterproductive in another.

Nowhere is this more evident than in the natural resources area. The government's one-resource-at-a-time approach to natural resource problems continues to have serious adverse effects. The "national" policy has really emerged as an accretion of numerous individual decisions. This after-the-fact policy takes on some of the contradictions accumulated over separate and disparate decisions. This can be clearly seen in government subsidies for resource use and government energy programs.

Federal subsidies have often led to waste of resources, misguided land-use decisions, and degradation of the natural and human environment. For example,

- The government fails to charge the full cost of federally supplied water; in the arid West, the subsidized cost is about 10 percent of the real cost, which encourages waste of precious water;
- Grazing fees on federal lands are about 30 to 50 percent lower than the fees charged by owners of private land; this encourages overgrazing, which leads to desolation of native vegetation, erosion, and gullying; and
- The government has poured billions of dollars into development of the nuclear breeder reactor despite mounting evidence that the use of the breeder and the amount of the plutonium it will produce will be uneconomical for at least 40 to 50 years and may in fact never be needed.

Research conducted at the Energy Productivity Center of the Mellon Institute demonstrated how some of our federal policy initiatives have worked against achievement of least-cost energy for the consumer:

- Heavy government research and development emphasis has been focused on increasing utility-supplied electricity, despite the fact that in straight-cost competition electricity consumption would have decreased.
- Regulations have forced industrial conversion to coal as a means of reducing oil imports, despite the fact that at 1978 fuel prices our analysis shows that it was not in the industrial users' economic interest to do so.
- The most cost-effective opportunity to reduce oil consumption is in the building sector, yet government programs have focused on the transportation and industrial sectors.
- Controlled, artifically low prices for natural gas have created excess demand; this has resulted in over-use in the buildings sector because of assured supply to high priority customers and under-use in the industrial sector because the supply was not available. The Natural Gas Policy Act has increased that distortion by passing on the price of higher-cost gas to industry only, thereby encouraging continued over-use in buildings.
- The present popularity of a massive government program to produce synthetic fuels well beyond the testing of commercial feasibility is a further example of the propensity of legislators to enact measures that work against achieving the least-cost objective.[7]

Why has the federal government adopted such seemingly irrational policies? In addition to the one-resource-at-a-time approach, present national energy and materials policies suffer from instability in direction and funding. There is substantial shifting and even reversing of these policies from one administration to the next, from one Congress to the next, and even from one year to the next. This instability has, in several ways, delayed or prevented the action needed to make a smooth and expeditious transition to a renewable resource economy; it has made the long-term planning needed to facilitate the transition to renewables an empty exercise; it discourages private investment in the new technologies, processes, and organizations needed for a renewable resource economy; and it discourages the best researchers from devoting their talents to renewable resource problems.

The other major problem was brought to light in the course of the three-year interagency study that led to the **Global 2000 Report.**[8] While most attention went to the study's conclusions regarding population, environmental, and resource trends, perhaps the most important finding, which received virtually no attention, was that collectively the executive agencies of the government are currently incapable of presenting the president with a mutually consistent set of projections of world trends in population, natural resources, and the environment. In their efforts to link the information systems and computer models of various government agencies, the authors of the report were continually frustrated by conflicting sources of data, inconsistent variables, and numerous difficulties in coordinating the access and use of government data.

The United States needs a comprehensive analysis of material supply and demand over the foreseeable future and the formulation of a national natural resources policy developed as a joint effort by government, business, labor, and public interest groups. This national policy should be designed to provide adequate resources and resource substitutes for the future, stressing conservation measures while balancing material needs and environmental considerations.

Reform of our natural resources policies must not be confined, however, to the national level. It must extend both outward, to the global scale, and inward, to the state, local, and private level. With greater understanding of the ecological basis for sustained economic growth, new approaches to strengthen multilateral cooperation will become more vital. Indeed, a major implication of economic and ecological interdependence is that as it inevitably increases, the ability of governments to deal unilaterally with problems on a national scale will diminish. The growing scale of issues such as the loss of genetic materials, the conversion of cropland, soil degradation, and tropical forest destruction, and the inability of many Third World countries to deal with them, could have serious economic and even security consequences for the United States and other industrial countries. More and more, economic, social, energy, and other problems with an environmental or ecological basis within countries will prove resolvable or avoidable only through increased cooperation among countries.

The federal government can help by providing a carefully structured, conducive operating framework, but much of the action in the future will be, and should be, at the state, local, or private level. Many of the problems we face in the 1980s are most amenable to small-scale, fine-grained solutions.

This is particularly true of resource management problems. Energy waste, groundwater pollution and depletion, piecemeal urbanization of prime farmland, and degradation of coastal lands and waters represent an accumulation of thousands of small decisions. Certainly federal incentives, and requirements in addressing some of these issues, may be useful. It is clear, however, that federal actions would be insufficient even in the best of times. State and local and private initiatives and experimentation are essential to obtain finely tuned solutions to the diverse resource management needs of a very big country.

Emphasis on state and local and private initiatives can also help the process of consensus building that is needed to consolidate the gains of the 1970s. Too many people have come to believe that environmental action comes only after an adversary process has produced legislative or judicial decisions that compel federal action. We must increasingly recognize that state and local and private action can help to create the support necessary to solve environmental problems that are seen to be real, near at hand, and susceptible of resolution by familiar and accessible people and institutions.

9

PRESERVING
NONRENEWABLE RESOURCES

Resource conservation, as defined in the Resource Conservation and Recovery Act, encompasses three main categories:

> The term "resource conservation" means reduction of the amounts of solid waste that are generated, reduction of overall resource consumption, and utilization of recovered resources . . . (which are defined as) material or energy recovered from solid waste. **RCRA, Section 1004 (21) and (20).**

The first line of defense is waste reduction — simply reducing resource use by generating less waste in the first place. The waste that does result can be handled in two ways: recycling, for keeping the materials and resources in the system, or resource recovery schemes, for those materials that do end up as solid waste. The potential for each of these processes changes with developments in technology, economic incentives, changes in life-style, and changes in product specification. The goal should be to attain an efficient balance among them.

In a sustainable world, waste could be reduced to a minimum by redesigning industrial processes and by carefully planning plant locations to ensure that the residues of one process become the raw materials of another. Indeed, what we currently think of as waste would become through resource recovery a major source of high-quality materials for industry and commerce, diminishing the contribution of rising raw material prices to inflation and allowing virgin ores to merely supplement the existing material inventory. Recycling would become a central organizing principle for the entire economy; technologies for recycling materials and for abatement of pollution would be integrated into production systems and not merely added on to them.

WASTE REDUCTION

There are a variety of ways to reduce the rate at which materials and energy enter the waste stream. Besides conserving natural resources, waste reduction has the additional advantages of reducing environmental impacts and energy demands and providing a check on the ever-increasing costs of waste management.

The principal means for achieving reduction are increasing the durability of products, utilizing materials substitution, recycling or marketing industrial wastes, developing and using products requiring less material per unit of product (such as smaller automobiles), substituting reusable products for single-use disposable products, increasing the number of times that items are reused (such as refillable beverage containers), and reducing the number of units of product consumed per household per year (such as fewer automobiles per family). This section will focus on the first three, which appear to hold the greatest promise.

Increasing the Durability of Products

A complaint often heard from purchasers of houses, major appliances, or almost anything else today is: "They don't make them the way they used to." As recently as the 1940s, most products in the industrial world were being built to last. By the end of the 1950s, this was undoubtedly no longer true. Many people can empathize with Willy Loman, a character in the play *Death of a Salesman:* "Once in my life I would like to own something outright before it's broken! I'm always in a race with the junkyard"![1]

When something is "used up," it is generally thought of as waste and thrown away. Rarely is it recognized as containing materials and embodying energy and then recycled. But even when an item is recycled, a great part of its value is lost. The difference between the value of the component materials and the price of the item when new is the *value added* — the labor and overhead costs of manufacturing and selling the product. To retain this "value added" for as long as possible as part of the national wealth, society must design its products for durability.

There is no question that most consumer durables could be built to last much longer. Two basic strategies toward this end include designing products for longer wear and designing them for easy and economical repair or remanufacture. This whole approach to materials and energy-conscious design, known as *nonwaste technology*, is receiving increasing attention.

In remanufacturing, many identical products are brought to a central facility, disassembled, cleaned, inspected, and then reassembled, usually on an assembly line. This is a common procedure with automobile parts and even tires. About one fifth of all vehicle tires produced in the United States are retreaded. These 45 million retreads have lifetimes up to 90 percent as long as those of new tires. Denis Hayes emphasizes the potential benefits:

> If all tires were retreaded once, the demand for synthetic rubber would be cut in half, and substantial energy savings would be realized. Jobs would be lost in the synthetic rubber and new tire industries, but new jobs would be created in the tire recapping business. Such businesses tend to be much smaller and more regionally distributed than facilities to manufacture new tires.[2]

Hayes also argues that the renovation of dilapidated urban residences, currently inspired in part by rising gasoline costs for commuters, can be thought of as an important form of repairing obsolete existing products. Often these structures are constructed more soundly than many contemporary buildings. If during renovation they are also weatherized and, where possible, outfitted to take advantage of solar energy, the energy benefits would be substantial. No new materials need be constructed for the shell of the building, and a considerable amount of transportation fuel would be saved as well by former commuters.

The concept of durability is not as simple as it sounds. A laudable aim for conserver technology would be to increase the average useful life of products, but this does not mean simply making all the materials in a machine tougher. The complex nature of modern technological devices is such that hard metals rub against softer metals, both come into contact with plastics and rubber, and so on. An item does not decay in a uniform fashion. A Canadian research team pointed out that the design problem is to ensure that replacement of worn parts be simple; the marketing problem is to make the parts available. It should not be a mere matter of chance if the soft parts of a machine are on the outside and easily removable; it should be a design requirement. Generally, products should be made to be durable, and failing that, they should be repairable. So durability in manufacture means either better materials or easily replaceable parts or both.[3]

Though providing effective rewards for manufacture of durable products is difficult, the government could consider a number of simple steps: setting of mandatory minimum standards for durability and, in some cases, testing by government agencies (analogous to existing tests for automobile fuel economy). Because automobiles impose such substantial costs in depleted resources and pollution, mandatory minimum standards for durability and sustained performance (including at least the engine and drivetrain) should be considered, backed by a federal testing and consumer information program.

The market imperfection of consumer choices based on insufficient or misleading information could be reduced by a vigorous government effort to ensure accurate advertising and full labeling of products. Full labeling would include the guaranteed and expected lifetime and the life-cycle cost of the product, presented as the average cost per year of buying and keeping a product in good repair over its life span.

One television set, for example, might cost $600 to purchase and $900 to operate over its estimated 10-year life. Another might cost $700 to purchase and $500 to operate over a 12-year life span. The first set's life-cycle cost is $1,500; over 10 years its total cost to the purchaser equals $150 per year. The second set, costing $1,200 over 12 years, only costs $100 per year to own. Thus the price tags the consumer should be comparing should say "$150 per year" and "$100 per year," not "$600" and "$700." If everything were priced on this basis, a revolution would take place in the manufacturing industry. Manufacturers would benefit not only when they keep their costs down but when they keep their customer's cost down.

The government could also choose, in certain instances, to influence consumer choice by altering the cost of energy or resource-intensive goods or activities — for example, imposing an excise tax on gas-guzzling cars. Or it could provide the public alternative services that effectively reduce demand for energy and raw materials — for example, mass transit is a public investment that helps reduce reliance on imported oil.

Utilizing Materials Substitution

The process of materials substitution as a means of conservation often involves reducing the material content of products. It is extremely complex. The traditional economic theorem that substitution is a function of relative price is inappropriate for understanding the process because relative prices may be only one of a number of major considerations in the complex process of discovering technical possibilities for substitution and implementing them. Central to the process is the comparative attractiveness of competing materials, not only in terms of price but also in terms of other factors, such as stability of supply, ease of workability, and tradition. Since raw materials are usually a relatively small portion of the total cost of the final product, nonprice attributes of the material and their effects on other costs may well outweigh price differentials among the competing inputs.

In many cases the driving force in materials substitution is the development of technology. For example, in the communications industry, technology development has significantly reduced materials requirements through solid-state electronics, microfilms, microwave transmission, and commercial satellites. This functional or system substitution involves finding a completely new way to perform the function of a component or system. The transistor, for example, requires perhaps one millionth of the material needed to make the vacuum tube it replaces. Optical fibers will dramatically reduce the demand for copper and aluminum wire. This type of process has become more important with the substantial increase in the prices of most basic metals and other raw materials. The area of functional substitution may well be a primary determinant of what our future way of life will be like.

Technology will not always permit an alternative material to be substituted for one that is becoming scarce. Nor will the needed functional substitution always occur. In general, the more technically complex the material's application or the equipment in which it is used, the more difficult it becomes to find a substitute. Palladium, for example, is the only material that gives adequate performance in electrical relay contacts in the telephone system. In other cases, substitutes may incur more frequent repairs. Many substitutions can be effected only at higher costs; otherwise the substitutes have been used in the first place.

Another cautionary note concerns the time required for substitution to take place. From 1945 to 1964 the average time from basic discovery to the beginning of commercial development was 9 years, and the period of commercial development was an additional 5 years, for a total introduction time of 14 years.[4] Equally important in determining the total time to implement a feasible substitution is the interval required for diffusion of a process throughout an industry.An international review of this question, which examined ten new technologies, reported that — as a rough generalization — a market penetration of 50 percent occurs in a period equal in length but additional to that needed for incubation and development.[5] Hence the total time required for effective substitution to take place via technological change rather than price induction, following identification of the potential scarcity and invention of an appropriate substitution technology, has been on the order of 25 to 30 years when diffusion time is included.

Substitution can take place in the energy arena as well. The greatest opportunities and results in conservation lie with using more energy-efficient systems and processes to provide the same energy services or benefits at lower levels of raw energy consumption. This means we must begin to look at energy not as a diminishing domestic commodity but as a service that could be provided by many competing sources.

Another route to follow is to substitute either labor or capital for energy. Recent studies have demonstrated, for instance, that labor is an effective substitute for energy. Thus, it would seem that in the present era of scarce fuels and high unemployment, policies such as price ceilings on energy forms and investment tax subsidies should be replaced by policies that exploit the potential for substituting labor for energy and capital.

Regarding the substitution of capital for energy, one study concluded that despite limited substitutability in the manufacturing sector, energy and capital do tend to be substitutable in the economy as a whole, indicating substantial opportunities for conservation through installation of more energy-efficient equipment. Moreover, it appears that energy and capital are especially good long-run substitutes. So it is likely that if energy's scarcity is reflected in its price, inefficient facilities will be replaced and conservation equipment will be used, such as insulation, heat recoupers, and automatic energy-monitoring devices. One study found that capital and labor are equally substitutable for natural resources in the processes of five out of seven two-digit industries studied.[6]

Recycling or Marketing Industrial Wastes

In recognizing wastes for what they are — misplaced resources — an increasing number of companies are beginning to reuse internally and/or market their wastes, in effect turning a strict liability into an asset. Indeed there is a growing body of evidence that recovering and reusing industrial wastes is both technically feasible and economically attractive. This can be accomplished through product reformulation, process redesign, replacement with more efficient equipment, use of recycling equipment, and interindustry waste exchange.

Union Carbide began to market, rather than dispose of, much of its wastes in the early 1970s. The return on investment has been terrific — every $1 spent by the Investment Recovery Group nets Union Carbide a return of $20 to $25. Monsanto Chemicals set up a subsidiary to market the millions of pounds of by-products resulting from its chemical synthesis process, which represent a potential market of $350 million.

The waste exchanges that have arisen in recent years are predicated on the old adage, One man's meat is another man's poison. What is waste to one company may be a useful feedstock for another company.

For companies to consider using a waste material, they must first know it exists. A waste materials exchange makes the availability of waste materials or by-products known to potential users.[7]

Waste exchanges are most likely to transfer wastes from one industry sector to another. Waste transfers take place most readily from industries employing large, complex continuous flow processes to smaller industries operating more flexibly with batch processes.

There are two distinctly different types of exchanges: (1) an active, brokerage type where the exchange actually buys and sells commodities for a profit and (2) a passive, information-dissemination type, usually nonprofit. Both types are needed as the first tends to deal only in marketable wastes, while the second can afford to deal in all wastes, trying to establish a marketplace for materials not presently reused.

All of these activities, both intracompany and intercompany, are very important because of their considerable potential. It has been estimated that the present quantities of industrial waste can ultimately be reduced by 40 percent or even as much as 80 percent. Regardless of the precise figure, all agree that the amount of residual waste requiring ultimate disposal can be dramatically reduced.

RECYCLING

No matter how heroic an effort is made to reduce the volume of materials leaving the economy each year, a large amount of waste will still be generated. In general, the most cost-effective and efficient way to reintroduce such materials into productive use is through recycling.

Benefits, Costs, and Practice

The energy-saving feature is potentially very important since one fifth of the total U.S. energy budget is now spent on materials production. Maximum savings from recycling 100 percent scrap would reduce energy output 47 percent for steel, 96 percent for aluminum, and approximately 90 percent for copper. Looking more closely at steel, even the limited use of scrap by the industry in 1976 saved 14 million tons of coal and the equivalent of 5.7 billion gallons of gasoline. Recycling can also have a favorable impact on environmental quality. When steel mills use ferrous scrap in lieu of iron ore, there is an 86 percent reduction in air pollution, a 76 percent reduction in water pollution, and a 40 percent reduction in water use.[8] Despite such significant benefits, the government has worked against recycling of ferrous scrap by subsidizing the use of iron ore with a 13 percent depletion allowance and has permitted railroad freight charges that are three times as high for scrap as for iron ore.

There is also an increasingly favorable economic dimension of recycling. Recycled materials have a financial edge as resources over primary raw materials since they are closer in composition to the final product. Thus they do not carry the high costs of mining, milling, and processing of ores and have less costs due to managing the waste and pollution associated with production. Recycling can be carried out in plants that are simpler and so require less capital investment and less time for construction than new mining and smelting facilities, and they can be located more conveniently. The operating costs of recycling plants are lower than primary production facilities, in some cases by as much as 65 to 75 percent. (A large part of these savings are the energy savings.)

Recycling, however, is not a panacea. It has some definite costs associated with it.

Most fundamentally, recycling like everything else, conforms to the second law of thermodynamics. Every time a mineral is recycled, some of it is inevitably, and irreversibly, lost. Recycling efficiency today averages around 30 percent for most used metals. Recycling also creates additional pollution and requires ever greater amounts of energy input "to collect, transport and transform" the scattered material. Herman Daly has emphasized this point:

> As we attempt to recycle more and more of our produced goods, we will reach the point of diminishing returns; the energy expenditure alone will give rise to a ruinous amount of waste heat or thermal pollution. On the other hand, if we recycle too small a fraction of our produced goods, then nonthermal pollution and resource depletion become a severe problem.[9]

In short, the introduction of material recycling permits a trade-off: it allows us to choose that combination of material and energy depletion and pollution that is least costly in light of specific local conditions. *Cost* here means total ecological cost, not just pecuniary costs, and is thus difficult to measure.

Because all other countries still largely depend on conventional sources or the supply of natural resources, a commitment by the United States to move toward an economically maximum recycling technology would establish it as the leader in this field and would result in U.S. stewardship over an eventual worldwide industry.

A considerable amount of recycling has taken place. In the mid-1970s, recycled materials supplied the United States with 44 percent of its copper, 20 percent of its iron and steel, almost 50 percent of its lead, and about 20 percent of its paper. Though these rates are fairly high, they had remained on a plateau for over a decade. Despite highly publicized programs to increase aluminum recycling, the market share for recycled aluminum as a percentage of the nation's total metal consumption in the late 1970s still stood at 20 percent, the same ratio as in 1964. Over the same period, copper has remained virtually static, lead and zinc are both down about 2 percent, and tin has fallen from a 29 percent market share to 20 percent. Thus even for a relatively high-valued commodity like copper, we are losing 40 percent of the supply available for recycling.

Part of the reason for this static performance is the low priority given recycling by industry. Only 2.6 percent of industry's materials research budget is devoted to recovering and recycling materials. In addition, there has been, until recently at least, a disproportionate amount of attention given to the question of legislating recycling systems for cans and bottles. Not enough attention has focused on the potential for recycling in major industrial sectors where the overall long-term impact might be even more promising. One commentator has put it this way: "We seem to have worried more about what the consumer does with his bottles, cans and old newspapers than with the need for large industries to base their production runs on recycled materials."[10]

Finally, it should be noted that because all of the factors affecting relative prices of primary and secondary materials are dynamic, the extent of recycling changes with time, in both the short run and in the long run. In the short run there is limited flexibility — both in individual plants in an industry and for the given installed technological mix in an industry as a whole — in using different proportions of virgin and secondary materials. In the longer run this flexibility expands as old capacity is retired and new capacity is added — with the mix of new capacity based on estimated relative prices of virgin and secondary materials.

Technical and Economic Problems
Inhibiting Industry Recycling

Barriers and Disincentives

Several problems inhibit the recycling of materials. In industry there are technical processing problems that have a common origin in contamination, which typically characterizes secondary materials. We also lack reliable information on the magnitude of the pools of the major secondary materials, so that we cannot determine the physically possible maximum production from secondary sources. Insofar as the public is concerned, the principal stumbling block to recycling has been the modern postwar habit to think in terms of "new" rather than "used," resulting in an emphasis on planned obsolescence: "use and discard."

The economic problem revolves about the fact that secondary materials are often used only as temporary substitutes. During periods of high demand, they are used to fill gaps in supply, but they are the first to go with reduced demand. Thus the prices of many secondary materials are more volatile than those of their primary counterparts — a substantial deterrent to investment in recycling.

In addition, the positive economic value of some secondary material waste is not as high as the cost of exploiting it, often for much the same reason that the value of some virgin material is insufficient to justify exploitation. The material in some postconsumer waste may not be sufficiently concentrated to be of economic value, for example, roadside litter. Or the material may be so far removed from processing plants that transportation costs would be prohibitive, for example, waste in remote rural locations.

Not only the positive economic value but also the negative economic value may be insufficient. The economic value of recycling material in postconsumer waste is the sum of the money realized from recovery of the materials and the money saved from not having to dispose of the material. While actual postcollection disposal costs in the Northeast may run to $15 a ton and provide a strong incentive to recycle rather than dispose, such costs in the West can be as low as $1 or $2 per ton and thus afford little incentive.

Discriminatory Taxation Policies

Perhaps the most important of the artificial barriers and disincentives to recycling are taxation policies that discriminate in favor of primary production. In general, it is common knowledge that the extractive sector of the economy is one of the most lightly taxed ones. In part this limited taxation is a result of special provisions for extractive industries, such as depletion allowances and capital gains for timber, coal, and iron and expensing of exploration and development expenditures. But it is also partly due to the special ability of the extractive industries to take advantage of uniform provisions in the tax code — for example, the foreign tax credit and capital gains treatment. It is now generally agreed that investment in extractive industries has been at least 50 percent greater (and possibly much greater than that) than it would have been if taxation of these industries had been on the same basis as other industries.

The three major subsidies for mining are percentage depletion, "current expensing" of certain exploration and development costs, and capital gains treatment of royalty income from properties used in mining iron ore and coal. The Treasury Department has estimated that the before-tax cash value of the three mineral industry subsidies is 8 to 12 percent of the value of output for U.S. ore and copper extraction.[11] Among the three types of mineral subsidies, percentage depletion accounted for most of the total value. The Treasury Department also estimated the combined (before tax) value of the three subsidies for timber at between 35 and 45 percent of the standing value of timber before cutting.

The general argument in support of these tax advantages has been that they stimulate natural resource development and thereby contribute to economic growth. Proponents also note that incentives for virgin domestic materials contribute to national self-sufficiency and security and improve our international balance of payments by reducing our reliance on foreign sources.

On the other side of the controversy, many economists and public finance specialists have long criticized these tax subsidies on the grounds of general economic inefficiency as well as tax inequity. The wisdom of virgin material subsidies has also been questioned in terms of their implications for domestic resource conservation and environmental quality.

According to these arguments, subsidizing virgin materials biases economic choices throughout the economy toward more material-intensive manufacturing processes, products, packaging, and consumer life-styles. As one example, percentage depletion has encouraged the growth of large vertically integrated materials companies that shelter their income by maintaining high prices for their virgin material input and allocating their profits to virgin material production. These companies are structured, both physically and institutionally, to use wholly owned virgin materials as their primary feed. They purchase postconsumer scrap only to respond to peaks in the demand for their product; accordingly, their demand for recycled material fluctuates over a wide range. In the steel industry the effect of tax preferences more than accounts for the difference between the cost of producing a ton of steel from scrap and the lower cost of producing it from virgin material. The net effect is a faster rate of depletion of our nation's mineral resources, increased energy usage, more extensive exploitation of land resources, increased air and water pollution, and a larger volume of waste than there would otherwise have been under a neutral tax policy.

Discriminatory Freight Rates

Transportation typically accounts for a very large fraction (often over 50 percent) of the delivered cost of crude raw materials like mineral ores, timber, and most types of scrap. These basic commodities are shipped in bulk, and long-distance shipments usually travel by rail or water to minimize costs.

Ideally, competition among carriers would cause all shipments, of whatever material, to travel at prices that just cover all costs (including normal profit) necessary to ship the individual raw materials. However, to the extent that different commodities or shippers are charged rates that differ relative to the required costs incurred by the carrier, a condition exists that economists refer to as *freight rate discrimination*. If substantial and systematic, rate discrimination can be considered unfair to competition among shippers, and it can also contribute to inefficient allocation of resources among products, consumers, transportation modes, or geographic regions.

Recent analysis confirms that for the two largest components of postconsumer municipal solid waste, paper and glass, railroad freight rates do appear to discriminate substantially against secondary materials. For the third largest component of municipal waste and the largest volume scrap material overall, ferrous metal, there is conflicting evidence, but a possibility of substantial discrimination also exists. In the case of the nonferrous metals, ICC data do not indicate substantial differences in rates between virgin and secondary materials except for copper.

What can government do to change all this? How, specifically, can it remove the disincentives and barriers and in some instances actually promote recycling?

The basic objective for government policy regarding recycling should be to ensure that price reflects scarcity value and that economic neutrality is achieved as far as the production and use of primary (virgin) and secondary (recycled) materials are concerned. Specifically, the government can effect significant change through a variety of means: revise railroad freight rates, repeal existing virgin material subsidies, impose an extraction tax, develop subsidies for resource recovery, and internalize disposal costs of materials.

Policy Incentives

Eliminating Freight Rate Discrimination

Revising freight rates that discriminate against secondary materials would be a first step to encourage conservation of scarce resources and to provide appropriate signals for the marketplace to reflect true scarcity values. The estimated impact of eliminating rate discrimination on recycling is small — not more than a 1 percent increase in recycling for waste materials. Two reasons for such a small impact are that substantial quantities of secondary materials do not travel by rail and that estimated supply and demand elasticities for secondary paper and steel are low, meaning that these markets are judged to be relatively unresponsive to a decrease in delivery costs.

However, the estimates undoubtedly somewhat understate the effect on recycling of eliminating rail freight discrimination. For one thing, a reduction in rail freight rates would probably shift traffic toward rail, at the same time exerting a downward pressure on trucking rates for secondary materials. In addition, it is quite possible that the available statistical measures of supply and demand elasticities relate primarily to short-term responsiveness of these secondary material markets. If true, then longer-term responses, involving more fundamental industry adaptations and investment options, could be more dynamic, leading to substantially greater long-term increases in recycling rates than the numerical analysis suggests. It is clear from testimony presented to the ICC that secondary material shippers, and many users as well, believe that recycling will increase substantially when discrimination is ended.

Repeal Virgin Material Subsidies

A more fundamental governmental initiative to achieve economic neutrality would be to repeal the existing virgin material subsidies. The relationship between tax subsidies and material recycling has been extensively studied. As with freight rates, the general conclusion from several studies is that elimination would not boost recycling significantly, but again, there are, major qualifications.

Specifically, the studies conclude that recycling of the major materials in solid waste would increase by only a few percentage points, at most, if existing virgin materials subsidies were to be eliminated. One principal reason for this lack of response is that the crude raw material (mined ore, standing timber), of which the tax subsidy is a relatively large percent, contributes only a modest fraction to the total cost of the finished or refined raw material (steel, paper). Thus the relative impact of the tax subsidy on refined raw material prices is much less than its initial percentage of extraction prices. Another major reason is that most investigators have found low responses to market price changes, both on the part of manufacturing industries that can use secondary raw materials and on the part of secondary material suppliers.

The state-of-the-art economic analyses thus predict a positive but relatively small recycling impact from removing virgin material tax subsidies. However, these conclusions should not be accepted without some qualification.

In particular, the conventional econometric analysis underlying these market estimates assumes highly competitive industries, using responsive competitive prices as the principal means of allocating resources to the production of virgin and secondary materials and of allocating supplies of these competing raw materials among potential manufactured-goods markets. In reality the major raw material industries in the United States are heavily integrated "vertically" from virgin raw material extraction (both domestic and foreign), to final finished material, and often to final manufactured goods. They are also highly concentrated "horizontally," with a small number of firms dominating each material market. For example, eight major vertically integrated firms control 75 percent of the steel industry in the United States, and in 1974, 85 percent of their iron ore consumption came from company-owned sources. Under these market structures, published prices of virgin crude materials and of secondary materials may not reflect relevant opportunity costs or retain their traditionally assumed significance in determining raw material production and allocation decisions.

Furthermore, in two important examples of innovation in the use of secondary materials, the Garden State Paper Company achieved full-scale commercial production of newsprint based on 100 percent secondary fiber, and companies in the primary aluminum industry undertook wide-scale recycling of aluminum beverage cans. Examples such as these suggest, though they certainly do not prove, that if domestic virgin resource extraction were less encouraged by governmental subsidy, the raw materials industries might shift their investment and innovational efforts somewhat more toward secondary materials.

The general conclusion is that removal or reduction of existing federal tax subsidies to the extraction industries would conserve domestic natural resources, save energy, and reduce the domestic environmental damages associated with basic material extraction and processing. The final impact, however, on overall material consumption and recycling may be rather weak, at least in the short to medium term for which predictions have been made.

The Virgin Material Extraction Tax Option

If the nation should decide to pursue a more aggressive resource conservation policy, one option to consider would be disincentive taxes applied to virgin material extraction. Such a virgin material extraction tax would impose either a unit or a value-related tax on mineral and timber production or sale. Its purpose would be to increase production cost and market prices — and thereby potentially both restrain demand for virgin materials and indirectly stimulate secondary material use. Such a policy would require widespread commitment toward increased material conservation. It would operate in precisely the opposite direction from existing tax subsidies, which stimulate virgin material production, and would therefore represent a reversal in national policy.

If the policy were intended to conserve only domestic virgin resources, the tax would only have to be applied domestically; however, if the policy objective were to reduce domestic use of all virgin materials (both home and imported), taxes or other restrictions would also have to be applied to imported virgin materials and to imported goods containing virgin materials.

The net effect of taxing both domestic virgin materials and imported goods and materials would be a less material-intensive economy. A given level of GNP would require less in the way of natural resources to sustain it and would generate a lower rate of waste products and pollutants. In addition, energy use would be less, partly because material use and industrial energy requirements are complementary and also because secondary material supply systems typically use less energy than virgin material supply operations.

Much of the impact of extraction taxes depends on the role and responsiveness of foreign trade. If foreign sources of the taxed virgin materials are readily available at competitive cost, unrestricted by import quotas or tariffs, import substitution would partially or substantially short-circuit the impact of the tax on material and energy use. Thus, under free trade, many of the conservation objectives of an extraction tax policy — especially those related to waste generation and domestic pollution control — could be largely unattainable. Moreover, part of the price of using extraction taxes for conservation purposes would be a shift in the balance of payments and a possible reduction in the international value of the dollar. Clearly, in addressing extraction taxes policymakers would be well advised to consider imposing an equalizing import tariff on raw materials and/or rebating the tax for materials and products exported to neutralize the foreign trade implications.

Extraction taxes would be a major intervention by the federal government into the private market system of resource allocation. However, given a national decision to pursue a policy of material conservation, extraction taxes would be generally consistent with decentralized decision making and free-market resource allocation.

In contrast with other policy options for regulating virgin material production or use, such as production quotas or rationing, extraction taxes would preserve the traditional role for the private sector regarding how natural resources are to be allocated among products. In essence, national priorities regarding the quantity of domestic virgin resources to be consumed could be influenced through extraction taxes, while leaving choices about specific allocations to the marketplace. This would represent a minimal interference with the efficient operation of the market economy.

Since the full effects of such taxes have not been studied, virgin material extraction taxes should not be levied at this time. If after further study there is a desire to implement such taxes, their introduction should take place only after existing tax policies encouraging virgin material use are eliminated.

Solid Waste Disposal Charges

Another policy option involves the government taking steps to internalize the cost of disposing of materials. Presently, the government discourages the recycling of containers and paper products by assessing the cost of discarding such materials against general revenues rather than against the price of the containers and paper products. To remedy this, the government could establish a system of solid waste disposal charges, which could take the form of a federal weight or unit-based tax on products and packaging that would be charged to the producer of the item and tied to the cost of disposing of the item. The aim of this scheme is to create a financial incentive for manufacturers to avoid excess packaging and use recycled materials, and for consumers to do likewise, assuming that the tax will be passed along.

The disposal costs associated with a product — collection, processing, and final disposition — should be borne by the product itself as far as is practicable. Implementation costs will play a key role:

> If there were no implementation costs, the efficiency criterion would tell us that there should be disposal fees, just as there should be effluent fees for air and water pollutant emissions. When the costs of implementation are taken into account, the efficiency criterion sometimes guides us toward deposit systems, because they are very nearly self-administrating and the costs of implementation are internal to the product cycle and those using it. In most cases, where deposit systems are not feasible, the costs of implementing a disposal fee system must be balanced against the loss of economic efficiency from not having disposal costs internalized in the product.[12]

Although the full effects of such a change have not been ascertained, it seems appropriate that society move slowly and cautiously toward adopting as a general principle that the sale price of manufactured products incorporate the costs of disposal or recycling.

The preceding resource conservation policies were directed primarily at the production of goods before they reach the consumer and recycling markets. Two policies will now be examined that relate to the consumers' choices of what to do with products or packaging when they no longer wish to retain them, namely, mandatory nationwide beverage container deposits and deposits and bounties for durable or hazardous goods. These two policies provide a direct, on-the-spot reward to the consumer for setting a product or packaging aside for reuse, recycling, or special disposal.

Beverage Container Deposits

A *beverage container deposit* is a fee added to the price of a beverage that is refunded when the container is returned. The containers may then be reused or recycled, although there is no requirement that this be done. Mandatory beverage container deposits for beer and soft drinks have been proposed as a means of reducing solid waste and litter, materials use, energy use, and pollution.

Mandatory deposits would modify private sector trends in the design and disposal of beverage containers. The best estimates are that, following initial industry transition, consumers would pay a slightly lower net cost for beverages, indicating that less total national resources would be required to deliver a given volume of packaged beverage. At worst there would be little noticeable change in net beverage costs. In addition, costs of litter pickup and solid waste management would also be somewhat reduced, and the population would enjoy the aesthetic but nonpriced benefit of a less littered environment. These factors suggest that overall economic efficiency in providing beverages and disposing of container waste would be improved. Certainly this is another way of internalizing external costs.

However, against this must be counted the decrease in consumer convenience (generally considered the major economic benefit of disposal containers) involved in having to return containers to avoid forfeiting deposits. Those who feel that this (unmeasured) cost is too high a price to pay for the waste management and possible consumer savings and environmental benefits will judge the mandatory deposit system to be economically inefficient.

The experience to date with deposits in two states (Oregon and Vermont) has indicated high levels of both public acceptance and return rates. However, because there has been very little experience in industrial states, the applicability of this experience to a nationwide deposit system is uncertain. Thus before instituting national beverage container legislation, the effect of such laws in other states that have also adopted them — Maine, Michigan, Connecticut, Iowa and Delaware — should be examined.

If it should be decided that beverage container legislation should be adopted, it should apply to all sealed beer and soft drink containers, regardless of material used, except cartons and carriers; the deposit should be for a minimum of five cents, with possible increases scaled to the consumer price index; and the deposit should begin at the distribution-wholesaler level.

Bounties for Durable or Hazardous Goods

A waste management concept similar to beverage container deposits is that of a system of deposits or bounties for durable or hazardous goods. Under this arrangement a consumer would pay a deposit when buying a refrigerator or auto battery, for example, which would be returned when the item was turned in at a disposal depot. The system would encourage proper disposal of hazardous substances, such as the chemicals in the car battery. However, its impact on the total volume of municipal solid waste would probably be limited because these items would still have to be disposed of.

Deposit-refund and bounty systems create a "market" for goods that no longer serve a purpose for their owners. Redemption centers become the "buyers" of the used goods, and those who redeem the goods become the "sellers." The purpose of these systems would be to induce separation of wastes at their source and encourage proper channeling of specific wastes, thus contributing to the broader objectives of either resource recovery or proper disposal of toxic and other bothersome wastes. Placing a value on these wastes would also reduce litter and discourage dumping at unapproved locations.

There are several possible roles for government in relation to these systems. The most direct form of intervention by the government is offering bounties. Under this system the federal government would establish redemption centers funded from taxes. For example, Sweden established a mandatory deposit system for automobiles. A tax of Skr300 is levied at the time of purchase and is refundable when the car is turned into a scrap yard. Since the company passes on the cost to the buyer, since no competitive differentials among companies arise, and since the money is finally returned, this procedure should rate "supportive" to all concerned. A slightly less direct form of government intervention are mandated deposit-refund systems, which involve requiring redemption centers to be set up before goods can be sold. The government would require these centers to redeem goods when returned, using deposits collected on new goods to pay for the redemptions. The third possible role for the government is no intervention. Independent deposit-refund systems — set up by producers or sellers as a way of inducing the return of the used goods — are already in place to meet special conditions in the private sector.

Deposit-refund systems and bounties could be useful tools in promoting source separation and reducing improper disposal. Hazardous materials are especially appropriate candidates. The case for using these tools for durable goods, however, is less clear because most of the possible benefits of these incentives are already being achieved.

RESOURCE RECOVERY

Centralized versus Source Separation

Resource recovery facilities constitute the last line of defense against excess waste. There is a strong rivalry between the advocates of source separation and the champions of centralized all-source recovery facilities. Source separation advocates feel that centralized facilities are capital-intensive behemoths that produce little net energy and recover a comparatively small fraction of the material value of trash. They feel that all-resource recovery centers are only marginally better than landfills as a destination for whatever is not successfully recovered through source separation. There is a strong fear that economies of scale will dictate that huge units be built at great expense to handle the entire current volume of urban waste. Afterward, cities would have a strong vested interest in maintaining the same level of waste to maximize the return on their sunk investments. This could lead to official discouragement — or even forbidding — of small-scale community recycling schemes.

Proponents of centralized facilities believe that while source separation advocates have laudable ideals, their proposals are little more than naïve distractions from the real solutions. Source separation is fine as far as it goes, according to them, but it does not go very far because people will never change their life-styles and make the personal effort required for such a participatory approach to be successful.

They also maintain that source separation programs face problems in keeping down costs and obtaining markets for their recycled materials. Municipal source separation programs are seldom profit-making enterprises on the basis of the materials recovered alone. The cost of collecting, sorting, and baling the recyclables generally exceeds the revenues from their sale. Prices for recycled materials are subject to wide and sudden swings. It is therefore critical to the success of any recycling program to develop contractual arrangements for purchase of its recycled materials.

These are facts of life to the nearly 300 municipalities that, since 1970, have passed laws that require residents to separate their garbage and the 7 states that, since 1977, have imposed "litter" taxes to fund a growing number of government-run drop-off centers, collection drives, and education programs. Towns that counted on making money from their trash learned that selling is not easy. A government-subsidized operation in Boulder, Colorado, for example, turned its first profit — a bare $1,500 — in its sixth year.

To stimulate markets for their wastes, state and local governments are employing such financial tactics as tax inducements and even grants to companies that purchase either recycled goods or the equipment to process scrap. California, traditionally one of the biggest boosters of public sector recycling, is offering technological assistance to companies to encourage them to use recycled material. In early 1982 New Jersey inaugurated probably the most comprehensive state recycling law in the country, levying a surcharge of twelve cents per cubic yard on all solid waste dumped. About 20 percent of the $4 to $6 million expected to be earned annually will go directly, as loans and loan guarantees, to private recyclers and manufacturers that buy recycling equipment.

Still, no matter how much progress is being made in developing new markets for municipal scrap, public officials are going to have to do a lot more to keep the recycling drive moving. Currently, less than 9 percent of the salvageable glass, metal, and paper in consumer waste is being recycled.

Advantages of Centralized Facilities

The advantages of centralized all-source recovery facilities are clear. First, the weight and volume of wastes to be landfilled are drastically reduced. Though there is some variation depending on how well nonburning materials such as glass and cans are removed, the amount left over after processing is no more than 10 percent by volume, and 25 percent by weight, of the original. This residue is sanitized and is largely inert.

A second potential benefit of centralized resource recovery may be the production of iron, steel, aluminum, glass, and even paper from waste. Although the recovery and reuse of these discarded materials would significantly reduce waste disposal costs, the recent recovery rate is estimated at only 6 to 7 percent. A technically achievable, though not yet price competitive, recovery rate would provide about 40 percent of the metal, glass, plastics, fibers, and rubber needed each year by manufacturing industries.

The third possible benefit of operating such facilities is the energy they could recover. Up to 75 percent of all municipal waste is generated in areas with sufficient population density that the cost of transporting wastes to a central processing facility would not be prohibitive. Still, the institutional separation of energy generation by public utilities and waste disposal by municipalities would be a problem from both an economic and energy perspective. In the late 1970s the United States recovered only 1 percent of the energy potential of municipal solid waste while Denmark, which integrates the two functions, was recovering 60 percent.

The Department of Energy (DOE) estimates that 200 million tons of municipal solid waste, the amount projected for 1990, plus another 14 million tons of sewage solids, represent a total recoverable Btu content of 2 quads. (A *quad* is 1 quadrillion British thermal units, or Btu; total U.S. energy use in 1982 was approximately 71 quads.) Recovery of metals and glass in waste would save an additional quad because it takes less energy to recycle these materials than to process them from virgin ores. According to the DOE, waste-to-energy technologies already available could recover about two thirds of the potentially recoverable energy resources in wastes.

Mining this "urban ore" has begun. Five refuse-to-energy plants processing more than 500 tons daily were in operation in 1979. Industry experts expect that by 1986 about 17 percent of the nation's garbage will be recovered in 20 large plants and 50 small ones (treating less than 500 tons daily). In addition, Harrisburg, Pennsylvania, and Duluth, Minnesota, are the first cities in the United States to adopt codisposal, a technique pioneered in Europe for simultaneously disposing of garbage and sludge. In Duluth the thermal codisposal plant was projected in 1979 to conserve 3 million gallons of oil costing $1 million per year, conserve an estimated 1,000 acres of land during the next 20 years, and reclaim 14 to 25 tons per day of ferrous metals to be sold at $35 per ton.[13] In addition to these advantages, codisposal also disposes of waste products in an environmentally acceptable manner.

Three principal energy-harnessing technologies are commonly regarded as holding the most potential for resource recovery systems: waterwall incineration, refuse-derived fuel, and pyrolysis.

Waterwell incineration to produce steam — widely practiced in Europe — is a mature technology, although new approaches may be able to increase the efficiency of boilers. "Refuse-derived fuel" is produced by grinding and (sometimes chemically treating) the organic components of urban waste. The highly combustible product can be mixed with fossil fuels in conventional power plants. Pyrolysis — a technology to convert wastes into high-quality liquid, gaseous, and solid fuels — is not yet being used successfully on a commercial scale.[14]

A fourth approach to energy production from waste that shows particular promise for metropolitan areas with populations over 500,000 is anerobic digestion of a mixture of municipal organic waste and human sewage. The by-products are methane, which can be fed into existing natural gas pipelines, and a rich residue that can be used as fertilizer. The principal problem is avoiding contaminants that could poison the digestion process or that could pose hazards when applied in fertilizer. Also, because this is a relatively slow process, the facility would require more land area than would be needed by other centralized technologies.

The prerequisites for success of a centralized waste-processing facility appear to be:

- Using one of the simpler, proven technologies;
- Locating a user for the energy produced; and
- Designing a facility to process only a portion of the jurisdiction's waste.

The latter measure not only avoids waste shortfalls but leaves the door open to instituting complementary waste reduction or source separation schemes.

The speed with which we can expand our resource recovery efforts over the next five to ten years depends upon a number of factors including the ability of cities to work out institutional problems, the degree to which industry will provide markets for recovered energy and materials, and the degree to which cities can solve capital and financing problems. It is likely that cities will have a strong incentive to solve these problems as it becomes increasingly difficult to find land that is sufficiently remote and undesirable and as it becomes increasingly expensive to discard the waste in an environmentally sound fashion. The cost of sanitary landfilling, running at $1 to $20 per ton in the late 1970s, is expected to rise by $3 to $12 a ton, depending on the size of the site, environmental factors, and previous practice, as new federal and state standards go into effect. At these higher rates, source separation and resource recovery will undoubtedly become a competitive disposal option in many more cities.

A Joint Source Separation/Centralized Approach

It may not be that source separation and centralized all-source waste recovery are mutually exclusive. It seems on the face of it that if all the bottles, cans, glass, and paper are removed from waste before it is collected, centralized facilities will have little of value to recover or burn for energy. Some argue that the economics of centralized recovery plants is now so borderline that they could not tolerate even a small source separation effort: a bottle and can recycling program that was 50 to 90 percent effective might eliminate any revenues from materials recovery; a newspaper recycling program might lower the Btu content of the wastes to such a degree that the energy of the plant would be severely impaired; or a source separation program that reduced the total volume of wastes by 25 to 50 percent might reduce the recovery plant's tipping fees to a point where it was no longer economically viable.

These problems of potential incompatibility are actually less serious than they appear. The technology for extraction of recyclables, except for iron, is in its infancy for central resource recovery plants. At most such plants operating today, materials recovery contributes a very small amount to overall revenues. Many plants burn wholly unprocessed wastes and do not recover any materials at all. Thus a bottle or can recycling program would generally not interfere per se with a centralized facility's economic position.

The question of whether the removal of paper and other recyclables from waste in a source separation program would seriously reduce the energy value of municipal wastes is still open. However, EPA data suggest that the impact would be minimal and, depending on the type of source separation program, might even be positive.

The argument that source separation could reduce tipping fee revenues at a centralized facility below the break-even point is more compelling. However, it only holds true (1) when source separation is introduced after a centralized plant has been built: (2) when the centralized plant in question is processing all of a region's waste, or (3) when it has no access to additional wastes, either because transportation costs for such wastes are too high or because political jurisdictional problems are too great.

The best approach to developing a centralized recovery facility may be to design the system to work in tandem with source separation at the outset. This would take advantage of the strengths of both systems: materials recovery from the source separation program and energy recovery from the centralized facility. If the source separation program did not materialize or proved less effective than hoped, it would mean a somewhat heavier load on the backup landfill site. However, many other factors can also affect the amount of waste available to a plant, including seasonal fluctuations, jurisdictional problems, and the fact that many localities have only the roughest idea of how much waste they actually generate. In general it is better to plan conservatively and perhaps underbuild than to build a centralized resource recovery facility that might eventually prove too large for the needs of the locality and therefore be uneconomical.

Are there steps the federal government can take to facilitate resource recovery facilities? Three potential steps to consider are introducing government subsidies, reducing institutional barriers, and facilitating local user fees.

Policy Incentives

Introducing Government Subsidies

Subsidies for resource recovery are explicit federal payments or tax advantages that are specifically granted to promote resource recovery. These payments shift part of the cost of recovering materials or energy from producers and consumers to taxpayers. The subsidies examined below do not include assistance specifically for research and development or for technological improvement, although these are undeniably forms of government subsidy.

Table 9.1 highlights the ten principal types of subsidies. The ten subsidies share several characteristics, which allows for a number of classification arrangements. Table 9.2 suggests two possible arrangements. First, subsidies can be classified by whether they relate to *capital* (plant, equipment) or to *throughput* (quantity or value of material sold, purchased, or processed). Of the ten subsidy forms,

TABLE 9.1
Government Subsidies for Resource Recovery

Type of Subsidy	Definition
Construction and equipment grants	Outright cash payments by the federal government to private groups or individuals or to states or municipalities: reduces out-of-pocket costs of building resource recovery facilities or purchasing equipment
Construction and equipment loans	Loans by the federal government to cover costs of constructing plants or purchasing equipment: provides financing for resource recovery facilities when the risk is too high for a private lending institution or provides financing at a lower rate of interest than that prevailing in the market
Loan guarantees	Promises by the federal government to make payment to the lending institution if the borrower defaults on a loan: lowers the risk to the lending institution and therefore makes financing less costly or more available than it otherwise might be (similar to the one above in effect)
Investment tax credit	A provision in the Internal Revenue Code that would allow investors to pay a smaller tax on earnings from an investment in resource recovery than they would on other earnings: encourages investment in resource recovery facilities
Accelerated depreciation	A provision in the Internal Revenue Code that would allow depreciation on resource recovery plants and equipment to be written off sooner rather than later: defers tax payments to the later years in the life of the facility than would otherwise be the case and thus reduces the cost of recovering energy or materials
Tax-exempt bond	A provision in the Internal Revenue Code that exempts interest earned on state and municipal financial instruments from federal income taxes: enables states and municipalities to raise capital at a lower rate of interest
Industrial development bonds	Financial instruments that raise capital for private business enterprises but are nominally issued by state or local governments: allows private businesses to take advantage of state or local bond tax exemption and thus build resource recovery facilities at lower costs
State and local taxable bond option	Partial payment by the federal government of interest due on a taxable obligation: reduces the costs borne by states or municipalities of resource recovery plant construction
Cash bounties for recycled materials	Direct cash payment by the federal government to a private firm, state, or municipality engaged in resource recovery, based on the amount of recycling achieved: reduces the marketing cost of recycling materials and the out-of-pocket purchase prices of recovered materials
Tax credits for recycled materials	A provision in the Internal Revenue Code granting a credit to a taxpayer, based on the amount of recycling achieved or on the volume of recycled material used: encourages recycling by lowering tax liability.

Source: Resource Conservation Committee, *Choices for Conservation*, U.S. Environmental Protection Agency, 1979, p. 63.

TABLE 9.2
Classes of Subsidies

	Capital	Throughput
Cash	Construction and equipment grants	Cash bounties for recycled materials
Credit	Construction and equipment loans Loan guarantees	
	Investment tax credit	Tax credits for recycled materials
	State and local taxable bond option*	
Tax	Accelerated depreciation Industrial development bonds* Tax-exempt bond*	

* Subsidies marked with an asterisk are also credit-capital subsidies; they encourage investment by giving the investor a break on the income from the investment. The effect is to make financing available at an interest rate that is less than the prevailing private market rate.

Source: Resource Conservation Committee, *Choices for Conservation,* U.S. Environmental Protection Agency, July 1979, p. 64.

cash bounties for recycled materials and tax credits for recycled materials are throughput or operating subsidies; the remaining eight are capital subsidies. A second method of distinguishing among subsidies is by type of transfer mechanism, that is, whether they involve (1) cash payments (construction and equipment grants, cash subsidies for recycled materials), (2) credit arrangements (construction and equipment loans, loan guarantees, industrial development bonds, tax-exempt bond project financing), or (3) reduction in tax liabilities (investment tax credits, accelerated depreciation, state and local taxable bond option, tax benefits for recycled materials).

A third way of distinguishing among subsidy programs is to separate them into "short-term" categories. Subsidies designed to help overcome barriers to the commencement of resource recovery (examples are technical assistance; research and development; local implementation planning; and aid to newly developing, or "infant," industries) are short-term assistance; the others provide continuing, and usually much more costly, assistance over the long term, as is the case with capital and operating subsidies. All of the subsidies in Table 9.1 are the long-term type.

While it is not a good idea at this time to establish new long-term subsidies, short-term subsidies can be an appropriate and useful way of helping to launch resource recovery activities that will later be self-supporting. An example of this short-term approach is the federal program of grants to help local governments plan for resource recovery.

However, the final recommendation at this time must be that no new specific subsidies be adopted. Basically, such subsidies should be viewed as a last resort in offsetting existing virgin material economic advantages. In addition, when subsidies are considered in the future, they should be designed to avoid undue biases toward large-scale, capital-intensive solutions since there are significant opportunities in this area for small-scale and more labor-intensive technologies.

Reducing Institutional Barriers

Government could also help by reducing the institutional barriers that prevent increased recycling of municipal solid wastes. The solid waste of a single metropolitan area is often handled by a number of jurisdictions with conflicting interests. Many cities lack the power to contract for long-term delivery of waste; such contracts are often a precondition to private investment in recycling. Even where cities do have the necessary legal authority and where they face increasing costs for the disposal of waste (especially in the Northeast), they miss opportunities to recycle waste because of the inertia of their solid waste management bureaucracies. Widespread awareness of opportunities for resource recovery is the first step toward overcoming bureaucratic inertia and institutional barriers in this field.

The federal government could facilitate movement in this direction by making grants to competing municipalities to help them figure out how to switch from solid waste disposal to resource recovery in the manner most suited to their individual community needs. Such planning grants are essential because before cities can justify making capital expenditures, they have to figure out, first, how to overcome the technical, marketing, financial, legal, and organizational barriers.

The federal government could also consider eliminating its disincentives, in the form of tax and revenue-sharing policies, that have prevented communities and citizens from giving serious consideration to the adoption of local user fees for financing solid waste management. This would allow communities to make an unbiased decision about the economic and social merits of having citizens pay for that proportion of the municipal disposal services that they actually use.

Facilitating Local User Fees

Local solid waste user fees are charges paid by users of municipal solid waste collection and disposal services that relate directly to the amount of services provided. If a household discards less waste, it would pay less for waste management services. Several researchers have hypothesized that the widespread introduction of quantity-based solid waste user fees could have important implications for resource conservation by providing an economic incentive to households and commercial establishments to reduce waste and increase recycling. In theory at least, it is possible to set the fees so that consumers have an incentive to choose less wasteful products and households are encouraged to recycle newspapers, bottles, and cans and to compost, thus reducing waste.

Although local user fees and a national solid waste disposal charge are both methods of adding in the costs of solid waste management services, they differ in several important respects: in their point of application, in the level of government that applies them, in how closely the charges can reflect the costs they are intended to cover, and in the incentives they create to change the use of materials in the nation. The principal difference between local user fees and solid waste disposal charges is their point of application: rather than a charge being levied when a product is discarded, the disposal charge would incorporate the cost of disposal into the price of a product. Another key difference is that the local user fee encourages recycling by charging consumers for the materials they do not recycle; the disposal charge encourages recycling by charging only when primary materials are used, thereby changing the relative prices of primary and secondary materials.

Based on the evidence that variable fees may encourage more economical use of solid waste management services, local user fees for solid waste management should be seriously considered by all cities and communities. In addition, there should be further study of federal policies that inhibit local user fees, including the nondeductibility of fees for federal personal income tax purposes and the current exclusion of user fees from the local tax base calculation used for federal revenue sharing. Finally, although the present state of knowledge makes it premature to create positive incentives for local governments to adopt user fees for solid waste management, the federal government should provide localities with information and/or technical assistance on local user fees.

A multifaceted, flexible approach to resource recovery is needed. Single-issue solutions, such as energy recovery or waste disposal for its own sake, should be avoided. To be effective and efficient a national strategy should emphasize a variety of means (from among waste reduction, source separation, and mixed-waste–processing options), diversity of local opportunity, and flexibility to change over time with shifts in markets and technologies.

The federal role should be limited to correcting imperfections in the market system and modifying government-induced distortions that discriminate against resource recovery and waste reduction. Simply put, the strategy should reflect an economic logic that stresses the use of market forces and local decision making and strives for efficiency in government and in the overall economy.

10

DEVELOPING THE
RENEWABLE RESOURCE BASE

Until quite recently people subsisted mainly on the basis of renewable resources: agricultural products, firewood, simple devices for the generation of wind and water power. The majority of the human population still does so today. But with the impetus of the Industrial Revolution two centuries ago, the new industrial societies have been fed not essentially by the annual bounty of nature as in the past but additionally by the consumption of vast amounts of nonrenewable minerals and fossil fuels. These new sources of energy influenced human development not only through use in industrial processes but also through modification of the way renewable resources were used. Harlan Cleveland and Alexander King cite a number of examples:

> The traditional vegetable and animal fibers, for example, were increasingly replaced or extended by synthetics manufactured from coal and petrochemicals, altering the patterns of consumption, land use, international trade, and the distribution of wealth. Exotic foods from around the world were transported to metropolitan centers in ships, trains, and trucks powered by fossil fuels. Even in agriculture, profound changes have resulted from the use of oil-driven tractors and other farm machinery, synthetic fertilizers, and a wide range of agricultural chemicals derived, once again, from fossil fuels; these now contribute a considerable proportion of the total energy input to food production in the most productive part of the world.[1]

Unfortunately, this pell-mell human intervention in the use of natural resources incurred heavy costs. Through ignorance, and lack

136

of a sense of responsibility for the future, early practices — clearing land by "slash and burn," overgrazing, and using damaging agricultural techniques of many kinds — led to desertification and environmental deterioration in many places. Shocking projections from recent studies such as the **Global 2000 Report** and the North-South study by the Brandt Commission illustrate the potentially disastrous consequences of present trends.[2] Both studies emphasize that the wise management of renewable resources is the key for survival.

Reports such as these and general mounting statistical evidence mandate a reassessment of economic needs and of the ways of meeting them so as to reduce reliance on resources that might be near exhaustion or that at a minimum will become more and more costly in the future. Economic practices need to be modified so as to better use the renewable resources provided, and continuously regenerated, by a bountiful nature. Perhaps then the bioproductivity of the planet could be preserved, and indeed enhanced, to ensure ongoing renewal. A shift in perspective did ocur in the 1970s that makes renewable processes suddenly seem fresh, attractive, and much more important in the near-term future than in the recent past.

Developing the renewable resource base will involve both investing in, and judiciously managing, the renewable resource base. In the past some federal resource management policies have reflected a philosophy that has encouraged short-term exploitation rather than promoted long-term sustainability of our renewable resources. That exploitive era must be put behind us. These heritage lands must be managed for many public uses, balancing needs for income, recreation, wilderness values, and resource productivity.

We need a national commitment to intense management and careful stewardship of our public lands. We need new programs to invest in upgrading their productivity. By making such a commitment, the federal government would create jobs, provide income for investment, and contribute greatly to the social stability and future economic health of all citizens.

The task of wise management, however, is far from simple. If each resource were confined to its own narrowly proscribed area, exclusive of all the others, managing each would be simple. But such is not the case. Mostly, they are mixed together. Land that grows trees for timber or forage for livestock also provides habitat for wildlife, stores and filters water, and serves as the base and backdrop for many kinds of recreation. It may also be underlaid with precious minerals. Any one resource cannot be managed with blinders on because what is done to or for it will inevitably affect some or all of the others. What will harvesting timber on a certain mountainside do, for example, to the wildlife that live on it?

Sometimes specific management practices may be complementary for two or more resources. Indeed, cutting timber often does provide more food and cover for certain wildlife species. But other resource actions are conflicting or competitive: building a new logging road may reduce the water quality in an adjacent stream. To further complicate the situation, a single action may have both good and bad side effects: the increased wildlife cover left after timber harvesting may represent a serious fire hazard. Analyzing such interactions is tremendously complex and is, in fact, the very basis for modern multiresource management.

Fortunately, a new approach to management of resources has begun — the application of systems science to problems of total or integrated natural resource management. The conventional approach has been to examine the possibilities of particular crops, wastes, devices, or processes in isolation from each other, with little attention given to the management problems of resource utilization, the economic balance, or the energy flow. The systems approach tends to focus on the whole utilization of the biomass available to a particular community, including interactions of the constituent processes, with the central objective of providing optimum outputs of food, energy, and fertilizers in an indefinitely sustainable system.

The adjectives *holistic* and *integrative* have very special significances in the use and management of natural resources. When it comes to the use of resources, it is necessary to consider them all: agricultural products, forests, soils, water, microorganisms, plants, animals, men and women. In any particular development program, only an integrated approach can make optimum use of the resources. Cleveland and King provide an example of how such an integrated approach may look: consider food and energy requirements together; arrange for full use to be made of "wastes" and "residues"; include traditional agriculture in the community's planning; maintain soil fertility and humus content; explore food addition possibilities through fermentation and the use of plants not commonly consumed; use plant, animal, and human wastes to generate biogas for cooking, lighting, refrigeration, and distillation; develop algal and fish culture; invent or adopt simple solar and wind power devices; and so on almost without end. They conclude:

An integrated plan will include careful appreciation of the carrying capacity of the soil, so that its fertility can be maintained indefinitely, as well as of methods for augmenting it, for example by inoculation with nitrogen-fixing bacteria. It will consider the energy balance to ensure that the net energy balance is positive. And it will look to the preservation of the environment, locally and globally, in recognition of the place of man in the ecosystem, living in mandatory symbiosis with all the species of creation.[3]

In the late 1970s California established a comprehensive program, *Investing for Prosperity*, for enhancing its natural resources. The four guiding principles that constitute the philosophy of is program apply equally well to the type of national commitment being examined in this chapter.

- The recognition that biological, water, and earth resources are the real wealth of our State and thus the basis from which our common good is derived.
- The assertion that government has a duty to maintain the productivity of these natural assets — a duty to posterity, of which the highest purpose is to provide for the common good of not only the present generation, but future generations as well.
- The gift of hope for the future made possible by assuring that our citizens will always have adequate resources available for the pursuit of a just, decent living in a prosperous economy.
- The assurance that the treasures of our natural and cultural heritage will be protected. These treasures, be they rare life habitat, majestic vistas, productive forests and croplands, parks or wilderness, healthy fisheries, works of art, or examples of outstanding architecture, must be carefully managed so that they can be passed on to enhance the quality of life and the economic security of future generations in our civilization.[4]

A RENEWABLE-RESOURCES TRUST FUND

For the United States to make the transition to a renewable resources economy, a full-scale, comprehensive, integrated program with its own sufficient funding base will have to be initiated. Lewis

Perelman has developed the conceptual model of such a program, which is highly innovative. Though one may not agree with some of its specific features, it deserves serious consideration as the type of bold, comprehensive approach that is needed.

Perelman proposes the creation of a national renewable-resources trust fund (RRTF) to finance and manage the transition to a renewable resource, sustained-growth economy. In his words:

> The principal source of revenue for the RRTF would be severance and excise taxes on the exploitation of nonrenewable resources. The most important of these would be a severance tax on domestic petroleum and natural gas and an excise tax (or tariff) on imports of these fuels. The tax would be on the order of 10 percent of the market price and would be imposed at the point of production for domestic sources and at the point of delivery for imports.
>
> A national renewable-resources administration (NRRA) would be created to administer the RRTF. The NRRA would have the same independent status as such federal agencies as NASA, the National Science Foundation, and the Federal Reserve, and would lead and coordinate the activities of other federal agencies concerned with renewable resources. . . . The establishment of the RRTF would hasten and ease the transition to a renewable-resources economy through three basic mechanisms. . . .
>
> First, the severance or excise taxes used to finance the RRTF would increase the price of nonrenewables. This would tend to make renewable alternatives (including conservation) relatively more attractive. . . .
>
> Second, the RRTF program would include tax expenditures (that is, credits, exemptions, or deductions) to promote RRTF goals. Specifically, these would be (1) exemptions or reductions in RRTF taxes on renewables to the extent that these are used in a manner to preserve their renewability; (2) possible exemptions or reductions in RRTF taxes on nonrenewables, where these are used in a manner to promote the transition to renewables (for example, nonrenewable materials used in the manufacture of solar collectors); and (3) credits or deductions for private-sector investments in renewable-resource R & D directed at product development.
>
> Third, expenditures from the RRTF itself would be used in several ways to accelerate and facilitate the transition to renewables: subsidizing renewables, supporting research, promoting adoption of renewable systems, and assisting other countries and the domestic poor.[5]

The RRTF could support a wide variety of renewable resource–promoting activities: grants for energy conservation investments; grants or subsidies for cost-effective solar applications; incentives for recycling; investments in soil conservation and forest and fishery management; utility transition assistance (such as funding to provide incentives for innovative rate structures); facilitation of adoption of conservation and solar sources; funding for long-term R & D focused on basic research and generic technology-development problems; grants to state and local governments (they would receive a substantial proportion of the revenues to reflect the highly decentralized and diversified nature of solar-renewable resources and the need for local guidance in the development of appropriate renewable technologies); and, finally, what Perelman says is perhaps the most important program, model-communities projects involving the design and construction of full-scale communities based on maximum use of solar and renewable resources (to provide "living models of the future").

Perelman cites several advantages of the RRTF over the existing federal government approach to renewable resources development:

- Users of nonrenewables subsidize users of renewables.
- Users of nonrenewables pay more of the cost of resource replacement.
- Funding for renewables development is approximately proportional to need.
- Pork-barrel expenditures on low-priority or unproductive renewables projects are discouraged.
- Business investment in renewables production and application is encouraged.
- Decentralization of programs to state and local levels ensures diversity and relevance of renewables development to local and regional needs.
- Earmarked funding for the RRTF implies less impact on perceived general tax burden, no deficit funding for renewables programs, and hence reduced resistance to public investment in renewables development.

Is the establishment of such a major trust fund feasible? Would it work? The best support for an affirmative answer to these questions is that similar programs exist and are operating effectively. Public trust funds have been relied on for many years in the United States and elsewhere as a means to provide for stable, long-term investment to meet important public needs. The best example is the federal Highway Trust Fund, which was established to ensure ongoing funding on the building and maintenance of the nation's highways.

Of even greater relevance to this proposal is the fact that several state programs based on severance taxes on energy resources and trust funds for long-term development needs already exist. In 1981, 11 states had severance taxes on coal, and 4 of these had established permanent trust funds. The purpose of these trust funds is to provide for general economic development and the development of renewable energy systems after nonrenewable energy resources begin to decline.

RENEWABLE ENERGY

The fear of running out of energy has a social, not a rational, base. Modern citizens have become so accustomed to fossil fuels and so transfixed by the necessity of building vast electricity systems that they simply do not see that their whole life is surrounded by a multiplicity and variety of energy reserves that not only exceed all present sources but have a further advantage: they are not exhausted by use. The technologies for new energy patterns are available, will become cheaper, and could even lead to a more humane and civilized mode of existence.

With rising prices and shrinking reserves, all of the new possibilities — sun, wind, water, plants — can begin to enter public use. There are, at last, signs that the public is becoming more receptive. For instance, the second-fastest–growing energy source in the United States has been grassroots renewable energy programs. A particularly dramatic example is that in the last half of the 1970s, with no subsidies, wood burning alone delivered about twice as much annual energy as nuclear power. As all the renewable energy technologies begin to take hold, the effects may go much further than the provision of energy. They may well imply profound and beneficent changes, giving choice, variety, and safe options to the central process of energy use.

All renewable forms of energy are basically derivations of solar energy. Some, such as solar collectors and photovoltaic cells, are more directly associated in the public's mind with the sun's power since they capture it directly through manufactured technologies. Though the potential from such technologies is considerable, they will not be discussed — nor will the use of wind power, geothermal energy, oceal thermal gradients, hydrogen, and so forth.

Rather, in line with the natural resource emphasis of this study, this section will focus on biomass energy — in the form of heat, steam, electricity, or premium fuels — derived from living matter (or matter that was recently alive, such as dead trees in a forest), the waste material from natural processes (for example, manure), or the waste from harvesting and processing plant and animal matter. Biomass materials include wood, grasses and legume herbage, grain and sugar crops, crop residues, animal manure, food-processing wastes, kelp from ocean farms, sewage oil–bearing plants, and a variety of other materials.

Fuels derived from biomass are becoming increasingly attractive for a wide variety of reasons. First, biomass is domestically available and renewable. It is also technologically feasible — a number of biomass conversion technologies are either fully commercialized or within a few years of coming on the market. Because many biomass technologies are economical at a very small scale, they appeal to groups who favor decentralizing the energy supply. Biomass energy is seen by many in the environmental community as a safer, smaller-scale, and more environmentally benign alternative to coal and nuclear development. Because biofuels can be supplied in a gaseous, liquid, or solid form, they can often be made compatible with existing combustion systems. Storability is an especially desirable property. Most renewable energy technologies, such as solar cells, windmills, and thermal collectors, produce energy only intermittently, and their use therefore requires energy storage. With biomass, storage is much less a problem. Finally, it has been argued that widespread commercial development of renewable energy technologies systems (resulting in local, self-sufficient, integrated forms of energy) could reduce U.S. vulnerability to a foreign oil cutoff and enhance overall national security in the event of a nuclear strike or a coordinated terrorist attack against a centralized energy system. In an increasingly volatile world, national security and renewable fuels development are a prudent and effective combination.

In 1980 energy from biomass supplied almost 2 percent of our national energy consumption or about 1.5 quads per year. Although most people would probably think first of *gasohol* (a mixture of gasoline and ethanol that is derived from corn), most biomass energy today comes from the use of wood in the forest products industry and in home heating. According to a report by the Office of Technology Assessment, biomass in the year 2000 could supply the United States with as few as 4 to 6 quads or as many as 12 to 17 quads (15 to 20 percent of current U.S. energy consumption).[6] The contribution will depend on a variety of factors, including the availability of crop- and forestland, improved crop yields, development of efficient conversion processes, proper resource management, and the level of policy support.

Of the high development total, up to 10 quads per year would come from grasses and legume herbage (depending on future demand for cropland for food production), and 1 quad per year would come from crop residues. In addition, various smaller biomass energy sources could yield approximately 0.5 quad per year, including up to 0.3 quad per year of biogas from animal manure and about 0.2 quad per year of ethanol from grains (approximately 2 billion gallons per year of ethanol or 2 percent of current U.S. gasoline and imported oil consumption).

Another, more recent study reached a set of more conservative projections.[7] It found that although the total 540 metric tons of crop and forest residues (dry) in the field has a gross thermal energy equivalent of about 12 percent of the fossil fuel consumed in the United States, the readily available residues could provide net energy equal to 1.3 billion gallons of high-grade liquid fuel (about 1 percent of current U.S. gasoline consumption), or to 4 per cent of the electrical energy now used, or to 1 percent of the energy consumed as heat energy. A major constraint is that although U.S. crop- and forestlands are extensive, only an estimated 20 percent of the total residues remaining after harvest could be used for conversion because of environmental vulnerability and the difficulty of harvesting some areas of land.

Wood

Worldwide, wood is still a very important source of energy. Nearly one half of the total annual world harvest of wood in 1975 was used directly for fuel. Such a percentage is paralleled in U.S. history, for more than half of the wood harvested from U.S. forests for the 300 years of U.S. history preceding 1940 was used as fuel. Consumption of wood fuel reached its peak in the United States in 1880 when 146 million cords (2.3 quads) were used. During the past 100 years, the direct use of wood for fuel declined to about 30 million cords per year (0.5 quad per year). It was used primarily as a fuel by the forest products industries, which used manufacturing residues, and for home fireplaces and outdoor cooking, which created demand for charcoal and hardwood roundwood.

Since the oil crisis of 1973, the use of wood for energy has increased. Perhaps a small measure of the interest in wood energy is reflected in the Forest Service's free-use program for firewood. Since 1974 it has granted free-use permits to anyone wishing to cut firewood for personal use. The results are truly amazing. In 1979 over 0.5 million permittees cut 4 million cords of firewood — seven times the amount cut in 1974.

The swing to wood fuel for nonresidential uses has also been significant. At least a dozen wood-fired generators are now being considered. About half of them have already undergone feasibility studies. The Forest Service has provided technical assistance to well over 100 industrial projects from public utilities to every type of small business. A number of installations or conversions have resulted, including conversion of brick kilns from gas to sawdust in the Carolinas; conversion of 20 megawatts of generation from coal to wood chips in Vermont; and conversion of two state hospitals, several school buildings, a prison, and similar facilities from oil to wood. All of this has happened without significant investment of federal dollars.

The Office of Technology Assessment (OTA) estimated that up to 10 quads per year of oil and natural gas could be displaced by wood and herbage by 2000, the equivalent of 4.5 million barrels per day.[8] The actual displacement achieved with bioenergy systems depends on the conversion processes chosen and the market for the resulting fuels. Gasification and conversion to methanol, in that order, appear to offer the greatest promise. Gasification is the more energy efficient of these conversion technologies, and can serve as a direct substitute for the use of oil and natural gas both for process heat and steam. Methanol can also directly displace petroleum fuels, although the conversion of biomass to methanol is less efficient than gasification or direct combustion.

The U.S. Forest Service has derived different estimates. It begins by focusing on the estimated 600 million dry tons of unused wood (1977 statistics) available each year, which is the energy equivalent of 1,675 million barrels of oil or 10.2 quads. The problem is that much of this resource is, by today's economics, unrecoverable. Many constraints must be overcome to turn the unused biomass into energy. For example, urban residues must be separated out from metals, plastics, household refuse, and other materials to provide a uniform fuel or feedstock. Residues from primary and secondary forest industry plants commonly exist in low volumes where high transportation costs may be required to get them to concentration points. Forest residues are diverse in species, size, and character; they are frequently found on difficult terrain; and they are often located in inaccessible stands. The economics as well as the mechanics of recovery of large portions of this unused biomass are unknown.

Granting such difficulties, if only 50 percent of this resource (300 million dry tons) could be recovered, an additional 5.1 quads of energy could be provided each year from wood. This added to current energy from wood represents 8 percent of current energy use in the United States.

The United States should consider a target of 5.1 additional quads of energy from wood for the near future. This will make a significant energy contribution, develop our recovery techniques, give us time to get a good handle on how much biomass we really have, perfect our silvicultural practices, establish energy wood as a forest product, and allow us to measure the socioeconomic implications of expanded wood use for energy.

Cropland

Both economic and environmental considerations weigh heavily on the potential energy to be obtained from biomass. Economic considerations center on the cost of bringing cropland into production, food price effects, and competition, both between energy and nonenergy uses of biomass and between biomass and other energy sources.

According to the OTA study, four major factors influence the cost of bringing cropland into production:

> First, the land is currently being used for some purpose that the owner considers to be more valuable than crop production. Second, an investment is sometimes necessary to convert the land to crop production, such as installation of drainage tiles or removing trees occupying the site. These costs can vary from virtually nothing to as much as $600/acre. Third, the land that can be brought into production is generally less productive, on the average, than cropland currently in production. Finally, this land also typically suffers from problems of drought or flooding that make crop yields extremely sensitive to weather (particularly the rainfall pattern). Consequently, farming this land involves a larger cost and risk than with average cropland; and, from the national perspective, using it will increase the year-to-year fluctuations in food supplies and prices.[9]

As a result of these added costs and risks, farm commodity prices will have to rise before it will be profitable to bring new land into crop production. Eventually this raises the cost of all farmland, the cost of farming, and food prices.

Increasing the production of corn for producing ethanol serves as a practical example. Except for land in set-aside (which is not a reliable source of cropland), the land that is available for additional corn production is not being used at the present time because the costs of converting the land and producing a corn crop are higher than the farmer is willing to pay, given the current market price for corn. This simple — and valid — economic relationship dictates that a rise in the price of corn is necessary to make it worthwhile for farmers to increase their corn production, and the amount of the needed rise will be determined by the marginal costs of production, that is, the costs of producing on the new land. The actual mechanism that will cause the price rise will be the competition between distillers and buyers from traditional corn markets, who will bid up the price until demand slackens or the price grows high enough to convince farmers to produce more.

When this effect would take place and how big a price rise would result cannot be predicted with certainty, but the OTA has estimated that a food price rise that is equivalent to a few dollars per gallon of ethanol could occur as a result. The National Alcohol Fuels Commission's contractor report on this subject indicates that food prices would rise 6.5 percent (or about $14 billion) at an ethanol production rate of 4 billion gallons per year.[10] This amounts to $3.50 in higher food costs for each gallon of ethanol produced, making ethanol the most expensive synthetic fuel. Because of the uncertainties about feedstock prices and the actual level of ethanol production at which the food-fuel competition will become severe, the economic costs of converting grains to ethanol should be monitored closely and the need for policy incentives reexamined carefully as production moves above 2 billion gallons per year.

As mentioned above, there are two main areas of competition. First is the competition between energy and nonenergy uses of biomass, which can affect the reliability of fuel supplies. Wood and plant herbage supplies may be diverted for nonenergy uses (for example, particle board, cattle feed) that may, at times, have a greater economic value. Adverse weather conditions also can interrupt harvesting or reduce total biomass productivity per acre. In addition, in areas where biomass fuels are just beginning to be used, imbalances can arise between quantities produced and quantities needed for consumption. Moreover, if any of these factors should cause bioenergy supply problems, high transportation costs or local needs elsewhere may make such problems difficult to solve through regional or national adjustments. Hence bioenergy systems that use oil or natural gas as backup fuels look particularly attractive.

Of equal importance is the possibility of competition between biomass and other energy sources. Generally, solid biomass is most economic for producing process steam or heat in medium-size industrial facilities where conversion equipment is operated continuously. Larger facilities may prefer coal because of its potential economies of scale, while much smaller energy users may prefer the convenience of oil or gas, if they are available. Finally, because biomass fuels tend to be bulky and to have a low fuel value per pound, their transportation costs, relative to other fuels, will be high. These costs and the dispersed nature of the resources may limit the size of bioenergy facilities to those requiring less than 1,000 dry tons of biomass fuel per day (roughly equivalent to the input of a 60-megawatt electric-generating plant). Therefore, market penetration would be aided by the development of reliable, automatic, and inexpensive smaller conversion systems — especially mass-produced gasifiers — so that small industrial, residential, and commercial users who are familiar with oil, gas, or electricity can switch to biomass without having to learn new skills or make major changes in their operations.

The exact price rise needed to increase the cropland in production by a given amount is unknown, but some things can be deduced from this analysis. During the next few years, bioenergy production from cropland is not likely to be constrained by the availability of cropland. However, the quantity of land that can be devoted to energy production without reducing food production is likely to decrease in the future. Furthermore, since the marginal cost of bringing new cropland into production increases as the quantity of cropland in production expands, the added cost in terms of higher food prices needed to keep a given amount of cropland in energy production is likely to increase with time. In other words, it is likely to be increasingly expensive to produce energy crops even if the energy output remains constant.

Environmental Implications

The environmental implications of biomass development are summarized by the OTA report:

> Biomass has the potential to be an energy source that has few significant environmental problems and some important environmental benefits. For a number of reasons, however, a vigorous expansion of bioenergy may still cause serious environmental damage because of poorly managed feedstock supplies and inadequately controlled conversion technologies. Also, some uncertainties remain about the long-term effects of intensive biomass harvests on soil productivity.[11]

The major potential environmental benefits of biomass energy development are the constructive use of wastes that could otherwise cause pollution; the opportunity to improve forest productivity and eventually relieve logging pressure on some environmentally fragile lands; and the displacement of more harmful energy sources, especially coal.

The potential damages from biomass energy development include substantial increases in soil erosion and in sedimentation of rivers and lakes and subsequent damage to land and water resources, adverse changes in or loss of important ecosystems, degradation of aesthetic and recreational values, local air and water pollution problems, occupational hazards, reduction in plant and animal ranges, and increased risks to endangered species. The potential for environmental damage differs greatly among the alternative biomass feedstocks. In order of increasing potential, they are: (1) wood- and food-processing wastes, animal wates, and collected logging wastes (no significant potential); (2) grasses (most applications should have few significant adverse impacts); (3) crop and logging residues (some potential for harm if mismanaged; speculative potential for long-term damage to productivity because of loss of soil organic matter); (4) other wood sources (high potential but theoretically can be managed); and (5) grain and sugar crops (highest potential). Wood, crop residues, and grain and sugar crops will be examined in order.

The use of wood as an energy feedstock holds considerable potential for reducing the adverse environmental impacts associated with fossil fuel use. It also offers the potential for some important environmental benefits to forests, including:

- decreased logging pressures on some environmentally valuable forests;
- improved management of forests that have been mismanaged in the past, with consequent improvements in productivity, esthetics, and other values; and
- reduced incidence of forest fires.[12]

If careful environmental management is not practiced, however, the results might be:

- increased erosion of forest soils and consequent degradation of water quality,
- significant losses in esthetic and recreational values in forested areas,

- possible long-term drop in forest productivity,
- decline in forested area, and
- reduction of forest ecosystem diversity and loss of valued ecosystems and their wildlife.[13]

The expected result of a business-as-usual approach to wood-for-energy environmental management would undoubtedly be a complex mix of the above impacts and benefits, with the marketplace determining the balance between positive and negative effects. Government action — including improved programs for local management assistance, increased research on the effects of intensive management, and increased incentives (economic or regulatory) for good management — may be capable of shifting this balance toward a net positive position.

Important environmental problems associated with energy production from crop residues are maintaining soil fertility and preventing excessive soil loss. The full costs of maintaining soil fertility when crop residues are removed for ethanol production are poorly understood and quantified. Nutrients removed by and contained in the crop, including any residues (such as corn stocks or grain straw) removed from the farm, must be replenished by some means if soil productivity is to be maintained. The quantity of nutrients removed in the grain and residue of major crops is substantial. Although the exact trade-off between residue removal and use of fertilizers can be determined only under specific conditions, farmers would have to increase fertilizer applications substantially to maintain soil fertility if crop residues are removed regularly.

Removal of crop residues alters the plant nutrient cycle through a second, less direct mechanism. In nearly all regions, removal of crop residues would exacerbate soil erosion by exposing the soil surface, which would then be more susceptible to wind and water erosion. Biomass conversion using crop residues would aggravate nonpoint water pollution stemming from agriculture and could aggravate nutrient loss and soil erosion. Streams, rivers, canals, reservoirs, and lakes could be subject to increased sediment loads. Beneficial soil characteristics such as tilth, water-holding capacity, and organic content could also be impaired. Yet because the environmental effects of biomass conversion are diffuse and indirect and occur over time, it is difficult to place a monetary value on them.

The major environmental danger from ethanol production is the large amount of additional land that would be placed in production

(20 to 80 million acres if all current gasoline use were converted to gasohol). Much of the land that would be used is probably now pasture or hay land, land that may have been put into this use because it was subject to erosion and because perennial grasses protect the soil. Forestland may also be vulnerable to conversion, especially because the clearing costs can now be offset in many situations by the value of the wood as fuel.

What does this mean? First, a large increase in corn production for gasohol will aggravate an already severe sedimentation problem in our nation's waterways. Second, between 10 and 30 million acres of forest may be at risk. Third, other environmental problems associated with intensive agriculture — including pesticide use (currently about 1 billion pounds per year in the United States) — will grow at least proportionally with the expansion in acreage.

To sum up, the expertise of U.S. farmers and foresters is likely to place a sharp upper limit on the level of environmental damage that might be sustained in obtaining biomass feedstocks. The extensive network of environmental regulations is equally likely to place adequate controls on the larger conversion facilities. However, under the present system some very significant adverse impacts have a good chance of "falling through the cracks":

> The "slower" impacts of agriculture and forestry — the slow but steady erosion that injures water quality and, over a long period of time, degrades productivity; the subtle effects of low level pesticide buildup in soils and sediment; the gradual loss of valuable ecosystems; and the occasional reforestation failure — are all likely to be aggravated by a significant turn to biomass energy use unless the incentives for good land management are strengthened.[14]

Several public policy strategies are available to reduce the environmental problems associated with obtaining and converting these feedstocks. For example, the problems with small-scale suppliers and users of biomass might be alleviated by increasing the availability of information and direct technical assistance. Because of the uncertainties, federal and state agencies wishing to promote biomass energy development probably ought to consider provisions for periodic review and adjustment of any incentives they offer. In the case of grain ethanol, for example, this reevaluation might occur when planned distillery capacity approaches 2 billion gallons per year — the level at which conservative economic calculations indicate that significant food price increases might begin. In the case of wood a formal review of the condition of forests and soils might be instituted when 5 quads per year of these materials are being used for energy.

In addition, incentives for environmental control may be strengthened by accelerating regulatory programs associated with Section 208 of the Clean Water Act for control of nonpoint source pollution or by directing tax incentives and direct aid to operations practicing proper site selection and management. Finally, R & D could be accelerated in some key areas, including: (1) design of safe small-scale conversion systems, especially wood stoves and furnaces; (2) determination of the environmental effects of certain poorly understood practices and technologies (for example, whole-tree harvesting); and (3) assessment of the effects of various biomass promotional and environmental control strategies.

Government Policy

Government policy must be reformed if biomass is to significantly contribute to the energy needs of the country without adverse socioeconomic and environmental effects. The government, first, should chart a realistic path for achieving a goal of obtaining 20 percent of our energy from renewable sources by the year 2000. In addition, it should develop a means of documenting uses of renewable energy by sector. The current lack of data puts these programs at a disadvantage in competition for research funds, in comparison with fuel production programs that result in visible and well-documented amounts of new energy.

Vigorous policy support will be necessary if bioenergy use is to reach 12 to 17 quads per year by 2000. This support could take the form of economic incentives to accelerate the introduction of bioenergy and to promote the establishment of reliable supply infrastructures. This is unlikely to occur until bioenergy attains a higher priority in the Departments of Energy and Agriculture, the federal agencies able to directly influence the speed and direction of development.

The issue of obtaining biomass energy from forests is instructive of complex federal government policy issues that can be involved. The value of wood as fuel alone can bring considerable competition to the forest products industry. A real energy crisis could push energy values to unrealistic heights. Government promotion, and especially incentives to encourage use of wood for energy, could create unfair advantage to wood-based facilities like power plants over pulp mills and even sawmills. The application of incentives to foster use of wood for energy must be carefully considered so that they accomplish their objective without adversely upsetting the marketing situation.

There have already been suggestions that the Forest Service could encourage more use of wood for energy by allocating certain portions of the resource for energy uses. This concept of allocation of resources for specific uses certainly goes against traditional multiple-use and multiple-product management concepts. The allocation concept may be appropriate in a situation where survival is at stake, but it may be premature at this time. A preferred approach would be letting energy as a forest product develop in a free market in which industry allocates biomass components to the highest-valued products.

Policymakers would also have to consider the massive buildup of the forestry labor force that would result if a year 2000 renewable energy goal were established. Many new logging, handling, and distributing businesses would have to be established, employing thousands of laborers, many of whom would be working in the woods for the first time. Equipment costs, in most cases, would be extremely high. Training and employment programs would be needed to supply the workers, and financial assistance programs to support equipment purchases may be needed to establish new business ventures in harvest, processing, and distribution. Government can play a role in such endeavors. Expansion of existing government-financed extension and technical assistance programs would also be needed to ensure that the expanded use of wood would occur in an orderly fashion without adverse environmental effects and with full consideration of the safety of the producers and users of wood fuels.

State governments can also play a critical role in expanding the use of renewable energy and associated technologies. Most have already taken significant steps. The first state-level solar incentive legislation was passed in 1974, when Arizona and Indiana passed property tax exemptions for solar devices. Since then 42 states have passed some type of renewable energy conservation tax incentive. Some 17 have enacted incentives that apply to both conservation and renewable energy measures; 25 have incentives that apply only to renewable energy. Leonard Rodberg and Meg Schachter have outlined the major types of incentives:

- Property tax reductions or exemptions. These are the most widely adopted incentives, with 31 states having passed property tax reductions for solar systems. Most apply to both residential and commercial buildings. . . .

- Sales and use tax exemptions. Nine states have adopted these exemptions for solar systems of various types.
- Income tax deductions. Nine states allow purchasers of specific solar or conservation devices to deduct the cost of the device from their gross income in determining their state income tax liability.
- Income tax credits. These measures, under which the purchaser of a solar or conservation device can deduct a portion of its cost — ranging from 5 percent for North Dakota to 55 percent for California — from taxes payable during current or future years, are increasingly popular. Eighteen states have adopted some form of tax credit, and the federal government has as well.[15]

A number of other financial incentives for solar energy have been passed in 11 states. These include tax exemptions for gasohol and reduced amortization periods for solar energy devices.

The most wide-ranging set of programs for promoting renewable energy sources were developed by California in the late 1970s. The purpose of these programs is to reduce the state's high dependence on nonrenewable resources; in 1981, 91 percent of its energy needs were supplied by oil and natural gas. Among the state institutions that have initiated these programs are the California Energy Commission, the Public Utilities Commission, the Department of General Services, the Department of Transportation, and the Office of Appropriate Technology.

In the biomass arena the state's Office of Appropriate Technology has demonstrated a mobile gasifier for agricultural wastes, and the Department of Water Resources has proposed a power plant that will use geothermal energy to boost the steam derived from burning wood waste from logging operations. Wood chips will be used to fuel the state's central heating and cooling plant in Sacramento.

California has one of the nation's leading solar programs. It was the first state to guarantee solar rights; and as early as 1977, it enacted a tax credit of 55 percent (up to $3,000) on the cost of a solar system. In addition, the governor's Task Force on Small Hydroelectric Development concluded that 400 sites in California could generate 500 megawatts of small hydropower given currently available technology, enough power to serve 1 million people.

Many other states are initiating similar efforts. Connecticut, as part of its comprehensive Winter Energy Plan, provides information, financial incentives, and assistance for the development of renewable systems such as wood stoves and solar hot water systems. The Connecticut Development Authority also makes available industrial loans for facilities and equipment that use renewable resources. Finally, low-interest loans, ranging from $400 to $3,000 and financed by a $3 million bond authorization, are also available for residential renewable energy systems.

If the United States is to significantly utilize renewable energy sources to replace current energy sources, not only the technological aspects of such a conversion but also the institutional aspects must be addressed. Planning for such a conversion should undoubtedly focus on minimizing the economic and social consequences that can result from changes in the source of energy and providing the necessary infrastructure to ensure its viability.

AGRICULTURAL LAND AND SOIL QUALITY

Preserving the quality of the nation's soil resources through conserving the soil and maintaining the amount of the nation's prime farmland are fundamental resource management goals for the 1980s. The United States simply must preserve its uniquely valuable capacity to grow food for domestic use and for export.

This is a particularly important time for a renewed commitment in light of the many pressures and adverse trends acting on agricultural land. Department of Agriculture projections indicate that the physical limits of productive capacity may be reached by the year 2030 or well before under a number of plausible conditions. Long before the physical limits of productive capacity are reached, however, the economic or environmental costs of producing food may well become dominant factors in determining feasible production levels. As food, recreation, energy, and other demands compete for agricultural resources, consumer food prices can be contained, and the necessary conservation and environmental goals can be maintained, only if lands remain available for conversion to agriculture when needed.

Fortunately, the American people seem to have a good understanding of the problem. A Louis Harris poll indicated that 53 percent of Americans consider the loss of productive agricultural land to be a "very serious" problem. The public seems to understand an old saying by Will Rogers that "land is something that they don't make much of these days."

Although many of the needed initiatives in preserving a sound agricultural base must come from state and local governments, federal government policies should be examined first because they are ubiquitous and hence have a significant impact on land use, generally and on agricultural development and conservation practices, specifically. For example, in the 1944-71 period there were 75 major federal legislative enactments, policy statements, and governmental reorganization efforts related to land use. Within the executive branch, 23 federal departments and independent agencies have programs related to land use policy and planning. The National Agricultural Lands Study identified more than 110 federal programs that might impact on agricultural land. Furthermore, of the 37 federal agencies whose programs sometimes encourage the conversion of productive agricultural land, only the USDA and the EPA have had explicit policies designed to consider the effect of their programs on agricultural lands. And even in these two agencies, some program subunits have not yet incorporated agricultural land reviews into their regulations and guidelines.

Preserving the Farmland Base

There is, at present, no coherent national program either to encourage or to discourage the process of agricultural land conversion. The main action that is taking place to protect farmland is at the state and local levels. Indeed the most aggressive options seem to be most suitable for states or localities that must deal with specific situations where the conversion problem is particularly serious. Nevertheless, if prime farmland conversion is a serious national problem, which it is, sole reliance on states and localities is unlikely to deal adequately with it.

At a minimum the federal government must cooperate by making its programs consistent with state and local goals. It should also go beyond this to provide direct support to state and local initiatives and to make sure its tax code is supportive of farmland retention. But first a look at the action that is taking place.

The farmland preservation movement can already count substantial successes at the state and local levels. Already 43 states have enacted property tax laws requiring farmland to be assessed at its value for agricultural use rather than for other, more lucrative purposes. Several states also stipulate that farmers who receive such assessments must keep the land in agriculture. Furthermore, more than 100 local governments have changed zoning laws to encourage the continuation of at least some farming. States have also employed such means as differential property tax assessments for farm property, estate and inheritance tax adjustments, direct marketing, state loan guarantees to beginning farmers, and restrictions on ownership of farmland by foreigners and corporations.

The following four examples illustrate the wide variety of approaches being used and provide greater detail on the specific approach being taken by certain states to preserve farmland:

- New York Agricultural District Law — Under this law, New York grants farming priority in the use of land and thus allows for the creation of agricultural districts in order to encourage farming and restrain growing urban pressure. The law is intended to "conserve and protect and to encourage the development of the state's agricultural lands for the production of food and other agricultural products." This goal is to be achieved in several ways: (1) lowering property taxes on land assessed for farm use; (2) restricting local governments from regulating farm structures or practices by ordinance; (3) where applicable, mandating that state agency regulations encourage farming; (4) modifying and restricting the use of eminent domain powers if actively used farmland is involved; (5) modifying the authority of public agencies that provide funds for public facilities and encourage nonfarm development; and (6) restricting the authority of public power/public service districts to tax farmland.
- Pennsylvania Agricultural Lands Condemnation Approval Board — Recent state legislation has restricted the use of prime agricultural lands for certain purposes, such as highways or waste disposal. An Agricultural Land Condemnation Approval Board reviews the requests of any state or local political subdivision for the conversion of productive agricultural land to such use, and only if there is no other "reasonable and prudent" alternative does the board allow the land to be condemned and taken out of production.

- Vermont Capital Gains Tax on Land Speculation — Vermont has engaged in an experiment of giving tax relief to farmers while discouraging the speculative buying and selling of rich farmland. Under the Vermont Tax on Gains from the Sale or Exchange of Land Act, a 70 percent capital gains tax is placed on profits from the sale of farmland resold within six months of the original purchase date. The rate of taxation on capital gains declines annually, reaching a level of zero percent after five years. The act has two objectives: (1) to slow the artificial rise in the value of farmland caused by short-term land speculation and thus to curb the increase in farmers' property taxes; and (2) to keep farmland in production by discouraging land speculators from buying farmland, taking it out of production, and subsequently selling it at a profit for alternative use.
- Wisconsin Farmland Preservation Program — The state of Wisconsin has developed a tax relief program to assist farmers and ranchers who want to preserve farmland. The program is open to farmers with 35 acres or more who agree not to develop their farmland for other purposes — that is, to use the land for farming only — for a period of five years. A tax credit based on income is then provided to the farmers. A state Agricultural Land Preservation Board works with county governments to certify and approve applications, and the program is administered by the state Department of Agriculture.[16]

The federal government could do a great deal to assist state and local governments in developing agricultural land protection programs by providing technical assistance, data, and, where appropriate, financial backing. This program of assistance should include provision of information and assistance to state and local governments to rank local agricultural land according to agricultural productivity, probable development pressures, and other factors to determine which land is most in need of protection in an agricultural land retention program. In addition, the federal government could provide technical, financial, and educational assistance to approved programs of state and local government wishing to develop agricultural land preservation policies. For example, the Soil Conservation Service and the Cooperative Extension Services should improve their capacity, within existing resources, to provide technical assistance to units of government seeking to develop agricultural land protection programs.

Regarding financial assistance, appropriate federal assistance programs should be revised as needed to permit eligibility of local government units, including soil and water conservation districts, to receive financial aid in developing agricultural land protection programs. The federal government should also establish an Agricultural Land Conservation Fund to help finance state and local conservation programs, including programs for erosion control and agricultural land retention. Financing of the fund could be tied to major sources of demand on agricultural resources while still maintaining the competitiveness of U.S. products. Finally, the USDA should consider small matching grants for "capacity building" to state departments of agriculture (or other appropriate state agencies) that seek to manage agricultural land issues.

Beyond these direct forms of assistance to states and localities, the federal government could assist farmland preservation in specific ways. First, federal agencies should thoroughly examine their programs affecting agricultural land to ensure that federal action does not unneccessarily encourage conversion and to take action to mitigate the negative impacts of federal activities on prime agricultural land. One minimum requirement is that the federal government should not finance or subsidize development projects that occur on good agricultural land. When a development project involves the conversion of agricultural land, the application for financial assistance should be required to demonstrate that there are no practical alternative sites on land less suited for agriculture.

There are a number of other critical tax-related considerations. Most generally, tax provisions that affect the agricultural sector should not favor purchasers of agricultural land who do not intend to retain the land in agricultural use. Periodic review of the Federal Tax Code should be made to determine the desirability and feasibility of offering positive incentives for retaining agricultural use. Finally, federal action should address two separate problems with the estate tax. First, the use-valuation provision for agricultural land should be revised so that it no longer benefits large estates more than small ones. Second, on the administrative side, the Treasury Department should simplify estate tax provisions and clarify information to farmers, landowners, and tax advisers.

Preserving the Quality of the Soil

The prairie and forest ecosystems have been largely replaced by systems of human design: the agro-ecosystems of our farmlands. The replacement of naturally balanced systems by people-managed ones has been successful in one sense: soils have been maintained and harvests sustained over centuries.

But in a more fundamental sense, it has been disastrous. Often the principles that sustain the productivity of a natural ecosystem have been ignored, replaced by an agriculture that draws largely on a diminishing supply of fossil fuel to produce crops more economically. There are a wide range of problems:

> In our replacement of natural agricultural systems we have shown little concern for stability and longevity. The land has been cleared of its natural vegetation and planted with crops which leave soils exposed to wind and rain. In order to make up for the resulting loss of nutrients, we have had to use fertilizers on an increasingly large scale. The result, almost without exception, is that we have replaced ecosystems which had a yearly gain in topsoil with systems which have a yearly loss in topsoil. The complex natural system made up of many plants and animals has been replaced by simple systems with only one or two components. Self-regulating features have thus been destroyed; vital nutrients no longer recycle within the system, but escape to rivers, lakes, oceans, and the atmosphere.[17]

These problems can only be resolved by a comprehensive soil conservation effort. The frustrating problem is that the USDA has at least 30 different programs dealing with soil and water conservation, yet soil erosion continues at a steady pace.

Also frustrating is the fact that the two major approaches for promoting soil conservation — making conservation cheaper and making erosion more expensive — each have significant drawbacks. The former, which is the basis for most existing programs, focuses on making conservation cheaper either by providing free technical assistance or by subsidizing the conservation investments themselves. It can be very expensive and it is often not focused on the most serious erosion problems. The latter could be accomplished by (1) adopting laws requiring conservation efforts to be adopted on land with serious erosion problems, (2) by charging farmers for the amount of soil that erodes from their land, or (3) by paying farmers for the amount of soil they prevent from eroding. The first would be politically very difficult, the second would present significant problems in determining exactly how much any specific farmer should be charged, and the third faces the impossible task of knowing precisely how much soil would have eroded if the farmer had not taken action.

If initiatives along these lines were desired, there are some novel incentives that could be more closely examined. One would be binding multiyear contracts between farmers and the federal government stipulating that effective, conserving practices be used to receive benefits offered through specific USDA programs. Eligibility requirements for commodity price support, cost-share, and loan programs could be included. A novel "carrot" incentive would be for the USDA to offer a financial bonus to farmers voluntarily adopting sound conservation practices. The bonus could include favorable payment rates in the commodity price support programs or tax advantages. Alternatively, the USDA could enter into a contractual agreement with a landowner or farm operator. For agreed-upon financial benefits, farmers would be expected to reduce soil erosion by a given amount through specified conservation practices. Generally, the greater the reduction in erosion, the greater the payment earned by the farmer.

What this all boils down to is that our traditional soil conservation programs may not be able to accomplish much more. The significant potential, rather, lies in opportunities for spending government funds much more effectively. Our soil erosion investments suffer from a serious imbalance: slightly eroding lands receive most of the investments, while highly eroding lands, responsible for 86 percent of the erosion, received only 20 percent of the investments. By targeting the funds to achieve maximum erosion reduction, we could more than triple the amount of soil saved through the program.

Another alternative would be to break out of the mold of traditional programs and closely examine the advantages and disadvantages of a return, where feasible, to organic farming. Such farming uses no chemical fertilizers and pesticides but relies instead on natural manures and natural pest enemies. The return of organic wastes to the soil, careful rotation of crops, and the use of "green manures" (legumes planted in the winter and plowed back into the soil before spring sowing) can produce yields comparable with those of "conventional" farms.

One intensive study, conducted over two years in the U.S. Corn Belt, comparing organic and conventional farms on similar soils for similar products, came to the rather mixed conclusions that the organic farms did rather better in bad weather, that in a good year the output of the organic farm was somewhat lower than that of the conventional farm, and that demands for labor were about equal.[18] The significant feature was that the organic farms were one third as energy intensive as the conventional farms. Organic farms used 6,800 Btu of energy to produce a dollar of output, whereas conventional farms used over 18,400 Btu. And since organic farms often supply local food stores, mills, or food cooperatives, they can also greatly reduce the energy costs of food distribution. Another study found that while the cost of conventional farming — using highly mechanized farm machinery and massive doses of chemical fertilizer and pesticides — averaged $47 per acre, the cost per acre on an organic farm was only $31.[19]

As the cost of energy continues to climb in the years ahead, organic farming may well prove to be an even more economically viable alternative — not to mention the fact that organic farming produces crops of higher nutritional value and creates less pollution in the environment.

The government could support organic farming by encouraging the adoption of integrated pest management (IPM) practices. Specifically, federal agencies involved in pest control and other IPM-related activities could be required to develop and use IPM strategies in their pest control programs whenever technically and economically feasible. In addition, the federal R & D balance in this area could be altered. Very large amounts of research have gone into producing chemical pesticides — with attendant risks of dangerous runoff, of devastation to many local species that are not pests, and of possible carcinogenic buildup in the food chain. But comparatively little research has been done on biological control, in which pest predators are specially bred and released to control specific pests, or naturally occurring insect diseases, which are used for the same purpose. Both of these techniques are effective controls for the particular pests but harmless to other organisms.

FORESTS

Timber supply will increase in the next half century, but demand is projected to increase faster and there will be further price increases. Consumption of wood, in its various manufactured forms, has been steadily rising — nearly one third since the early 1950s — and projections indicate the upward trend will continue. During the next 50 years, demand for wood is expected to increase about 60 percent under equilibrium price projections: from 16 billion cubic feet in 1976 to 19 billion in 1990, and to 26 billion by 2030.

Assuming less land in the future for growing timber than is available now, how are these rising demands going to be met? If the present trend continues and future demand increases faster than supply, the two will be reconciled by an upward adjustment that will lower the demand and increase the supply until demand and supply are balanced.

Fortunately, there appears to be substantial scope for improvements in timber production. A joint study by the U.S. Forest Service and the Forest Industries Council, covering 25 states that contain 83 percent of the total commercial forestland, identified forest management investments that would have a return of at least 10 percent per year after taxes.[20] Making these investments would increase the nation's total annual growth by 50 percent, with the greatest increase occurring in the national forests. The most common and generally most profitable improvement identified in the study is the regeneration of forestlands with faster-growing and more commercially valuable trees. This is recommended for 72 percent of the 139 million acres that were identified as benefiting from some form of treatment and would take 93 percent of the total required public and private investment of $10.3 billion.

In this era of tight budgets, it is unlikely that anywhere near this much will be invested. Still, there is much that both the private sector and the public sector can do.

Private Sector Initiatives

The potential for increased production differs greatly between forest industry and private nonindustrial owners. Forest industry lands provide little potential because the firms both have the information required to make the investments and usually have reasonable access to financing. Private nonindustrial owners, on the other hand, have substantial potential to increase production. However, they apparently lack either the desire, the information, or the financing to do so. Hence public policies would be of little assistance to the forest industry but could be of great assistance to the nonindustrial owners (see the following section).

There is a large potential for both types of owners to extend timber supplies through improvements in use. The private sector should attempt to increase the use of wood by:

- Improving wood yields by increasing the use of residues in existing and new production processes;
- Improving the grading, engineering, preservation, and maintenance of wood products and wood structures; and
- Increasing the recovery of waste fiber for products and energy.

Logging and primary-manufacturing plant residues in 1976 totaled about 2 billion cubic feet. About 67 billion cubic feet of wood was represented in rough and rotten and salvagable trees, and dead trees. Large additional volumes were in tops, limbs, and stumps, and urban wood wastes. Although part of the available residue is in remote locations or occurs in such small volumes as to be unusable, much of the material is potentially suitable for pulp or fuel.

Another form of improved utilization is improved engineering practices, which could reduce the amount of wood needed in houses and other structures. Such practices could save, for example, an estimated 10 to 20 percent of the dimension lumber used in the typical framehouse. Proper use of preservative-treated products, insecticides to control termites, and careful application of water-repellents could greatly extend the useful life of most wood products and reduce demand on timber resources. Improved maintenance and renovation of existing structures could also reduce demands for timber, and other materials as well, below the volumes needed for new replacement structures.

Only so much, however, can be done through improvements in utilization. By far the greatest potential lies with increasing timber supply. The best gauge of this potential is that in 1976 average net timber growth per acre was 49 cubic feet, three fifths of what can be achieved with intensive management practices such as spacing control and the use of genetically improved stock and fertilizers. The potential for increasing timber growth exists in all regions and in all private and public forests. The largest potential for the long term, however, rests with the farmer and miscellaneous private ownerships, which collectively contain 58 percent of the nation's commercial timberlands. Most of these lands are advantageously located with respect to markets and largely composed of the more fertile sites used for timber production.

If harvests from industrial private forests are to increase, current levels of regeneration and growth must increase. Currently, there is a serious shortfall of reforestation following harvest. This problem is particularly acute in the South where harvesting will produce an increasing share of mature softwood sawtimber. The shortfall is caused primarily by the absence of planned regeneration following harvest on many ownerships.

There are many opportunities for investments in reforestation and timber-stand improvement that yield satisfactory financial returns. Most of these opportunities are in the South, but they are also found in the North and on the Pacific Coast.

Government Initiatives

These broad economic, social, and environmental benefits — and the likelihood that even direct benefits, such as income from timber sales, will not accrue to current owners because of short tenure or life expectancy — suggest two things. First, there is a strong justification for publicly supported cost-sharing and technical assistance programs. Second, existing economic opportunities for management intensification in privately owned forests are not likely to be realized in any substantive way without such programs.

Since the potential increase in timber production on state and private lands is the key to expanding the supply of timber in the United States, Congress should design a comprehensive package of legislation aimed at increasing the level of forest management in productive private forestlands.

Working together to implement this program, the Forest Service, the Rural Development Staff, and the Economic Statistics Service of the Department of Agriculture should design and test various strategies for the implementation of joint management ventures for private forests. Specifically, the potential effectiveness of profit-making ventures, nonprofit corporations, and cooperatives should be considered.

A complementary program should be implemented on a pilot basis to test a variety of incentive programs (for example, technical assistance, loans, tax credits) in different situations. Finally, Congress should request that the Forest Service evaluate a wide variety of methods of ensuring sustainable yields of timber from the nation's private forestlands.

Another legitimate function for government is assisting in technology development through expanded R & D efforts. Much can be done now to extend timber supplies by better use of existing technology. But, progressing from extensive to intensive management, there is need for a continuing flow of new information to guide along the way. More research is still needed on all phases of growing, protecting, and using forests for timber. Specifically, the Forest Service should accelerate its research, development, and application programs to expand wood supplies through improved technology and utilization. New utilization technology should be viewed as the most cost-effective way to increase future softwood timber supplies.

State and Private Forestry products utilization programs should provide technical assistance to emphasize the application of technology to improve harvesting, processing, and use of wood and wood-based products. Utilization specialists could provide assistance in a broad range of activities, from timber harvesting through primary and secondary processing and marketing, to encourage and induce improved wood utilization. Improved utilization of eastern hardwood can be stressed to increase the use of low-quality hardwood with resulting higher quality hardwood stands available as a future resource.

Finally, we face the basic question of how our public lands are to be managed in the future. Increasing production on public lands would involve, in some cases, substantial modifications of the current management principles of multiple use and sustained yield. While aggressive cutting on public lands would increase timber harvests and lower timber prices, thereby benefiting consumers, it would also lower the value of timber on private lands, thereby discouraging private investment in improved forest management on those lands that provide the largest potential for increased production. In addition, other uses of public forestland — recreation, wildlife habitat, water supply enhancement, erosion control and so forth — would suffer under a policy of aggressive cutting.

There are a number of ways, however, for forest managers to minimize the damage. They can retain the trees along streams to slow sedimentation and warming and leave corridors of trees through which wildlife can move; they can clear-cut in small patches so that forests of differing ages are available; they can leave snags and fallen logs, vary the species in the patches, allow some patches to reach maturity, stop herbicide applications after seedlings are established, seed the understory with herbaceous and bushy plants to minimize erosion and provide cover and food for wildlife, and use integrated pest management techniques rather than routinely spraying pesticides. These measures may decrease short-term profits, but they will also lessen damage to forest inhabitants and provide for sustainable productivity and, hence, longer-term economic gains.

To meet the increased demand pressures in the 1980s, primarily from housing, it will most likely be necessary to draw more heavily on the large inventories of mature and overmature timber on public land, particularly in certain national forests in the West. Perhaps the best solution would be a compromise between continuing the existing management approach and extensive accelerated harvesting on public lands — managing selected lands intensively for timber production, while retaining current management approaches on the rest. This "dedicated use" alternative, in comparison with current policies, would result in lower timber prices and lessened impact on wilderness and remote wildlife habitat.

WATER

The United States has a serious water problem. But the nation's water problem is not one of inadequate supply: it is endowed with bountiful water supplies that should be adequate for generations. The problem is that these supplies are being squandered through poor management and inefficient use to such a degree that water is running short in many areas. The waste is actively encouraged by outdated laws, government subsidies, and the complex political rivalries that have long surrounded water use. Hence the solutions to the water problem are not ultimately technological — though there is much that can be done to stretch resources — but political and economic. We are simply going to have to work out substantially new ways of managing water.

With the passage of time, various laws, administrative structures, and other economic and social institutions have evolved to resolve conflicts and act as instruments for allocating the nation's waters. Many of these were the outgrowth of local disputes and, at their inception, were adequate for the task for which they were designed. Unfortunately, water quantity was until recently (and even now is) often treated separately from water quality; groundwater and surface water sources have been treated by law and development as though they were hydrologically independent; and a host of water resources agencies have been established, often with narrow focus. As a by-product of the way in which our water policy and institutions have evolved, the resolution of many conflicts has now reached an impasse, and efforts are still being made to solve problems that no longer exist, while critical issues go begging.

Perhaps the most critical issue to be resolved is how to attain the most efficient use and strategic distribution of water. Since the nation's water supply cannot be substantially augumented, water conservation must become a widespread practice. Fortunately, there is considerable potential.

Conservation as a means of stretching water supplies or protecting water quality has long been understood. The difficulty is getting people to accept and employ the technology available. Specific long-term conservation problems include:

- Lack of comprehensive national water policy,
- The prevailing body of water law,
- Failure to recognize the interrelationship between surface and groundwaters,
- Lack of appropriate institutions for managing regional and interstate water resources,
- Lack of incentives for generating widespread implemention of conservation practices, and
- Failure to establish a price for water that is commensurate with the value of its use.

Faced with all these problems, there usually must be some incentive for water conservation to take place. Two kinds of incentives are commonly available: economic and regulatory. The more direct approach is to make it illegal to waste water. But this approach is less effective and more expensive than applying a more realistic pricing system.

A Water Market

The most straightforward way of encouraging the changeover to more conserving methods is to introduce water charges. In the agricultural sector where the greatest water use is, this would either (1) force farmers to adopt more efficient irrigation methods or to switch to more valuable crops or (2) allow the market, when the price climbs high, to divert water to municipal and industrial users willing to pay more.

There simply is no better way to stop waste than to introduce the discipline of the marketplace. New water projects could be avoided for years if the price of water were allowed to move toward its replacement cost, which is 50 times what some farmers are currently paying. Water from new federal projects would cost at least $160 an acre-foot if the price covered construction of dams and canals at today's inflated costs, plus the operation and maintenance of these facilities. But few agricultural users of federal water pay anything remotely as high. Farmers in California's Central Valley pay only $3.50 an acre-foot. This means federal subsidies of over $3 million for a typical 2,200 acre farm in California.

It would not be easy to create a water market. Indeed most states have long-standing prohibitions against buying or selling water. Hence it would be politically difficult if not illegal to sweep away the great patchwork of water rights granted over the years to farmers, cities, industry, and political jurisdictions. These rights, which in many cases still have decades to run, would have to be "grandfathered." Only within a context of grandfathered water rights could the law of supply and demand begin to take effect.

However, several institutional and historical practices now impede the quick and easy transfer of water rights to new uses. In Arizona, for example, groundwater can be obtained only by purchasing land. Throughout the West, contested Indian rights are clouding water titles, many water conservancy districts and irrigation companies are fighting state-approved water transfers in the courts, and the states are increasingly contesting the federal government's attempts — often made to protect Indian interests — to "reserve" title to unused water on federal lands.

The problem of surface water versus groundwater also complicates water transfers. The availability of enough water to satisfy an owner's rights may depend on how much water percolates or flows from another owner's supply. But title to surface water does not go with the land as it does with groundwater.

The reform of water pricing would cause widespread economic dislocation in the short run as marginal farms and other enterprises closed, as profitable farms were forced to shift crops, and as mines were revamped to conserve more of the water they use. For example, in Wyoming 850,000 acres of ranch land were purchased in the early 1980s just for their water. This is understandable because industry produces about 60 times the economic return per gallon as does agriculture. In general, though, the dislocations would not halt the Southwest's growth nor would they cause general hardship. Water charges can also be accompanied by tax rebates and depreciation allowances to cover part of the cost of the necessary changes in process equipment — a particularly important point wherever new water charges threaten to knock out the small plant while being comfortably carried by the large.

A water market would have one unavoidable complication: It would have to include strict regulation of groundwater usage. Under relatively free market conditions, farmers and other users would have a stronger incentive to use this water, which is often the cheapest available. Thus, any reform of water pricing would have to be accompanied by some kind of restraint to keep users from depleting the common groundwater.

Water markets already exist to a limited extent in the Southwest, although transfers tend to be expensive and subject to red tape. The first and one of the best systems operates in New Mexico, which permits the buying and selling of ground- and surface water rights among holders in 26 designated water basins containing 90 percent of the state's water. Once a basin is created, new pumping is restricted. There is, however, a hitch in this market system and those of most other states: it is difficult to sell off the "conserved surplus" — the water left over when a farmer or any other user manages to use less water than before. If there is to be a free market, users should be permitted to sell any water they have, conserved surplus and all.

Other experience with pricing does confirm that it greatly influences water use. In Boulder, Colorado, for example, the introduction of metering reduced water use by more than one third. The National Water Commission concluded that charging users the full cost of water services would conserve water supplies by encouraging more efficient use of scarce resources and discouraging premature invesment in new water development projects. It would also reduce the financial burden on nonusers.

Irrigation Conservation

Given the incentive — whether financial or legal — land managers and water users can conserve water in a variety of ways.

Perhaps the greatest opportunity for conservation is where water use is greatest: irrigation, which accounts for 83 percent of our water consumption. Current irrigated land exceeds 50 million acres or about one sixth of all land farmed. In 1976 total withdrawals of water in the contiguous United States for all uses were about 400 million acre-feet with approximately 50 percent attributed to irrigation; during that same year, total depletions amounted to about 125 million acre-feet with irrigated agriculture accounting for almost 80 percent. In irrigation large amounts of water are wasted — as much as 50 percent — during transmission, before it reaches its intended destination, either by seeping into the ground or evaporating. Such losses could be minimized by activities such as lining channels with nonporous materials, converting from surface flooding to drip irrigation, using underground storage in wet years, controlling water-absorbing plants that commonly grow adjacent to channels, monitoring soil moisture, and timing applications.

Estimates of water savings obtainable through improved efficiencies in irrigation water management generally range between 20 and 50 percent. Conservatively estimating just a 10 percent reduction, savings of about 20 million acre-feet in water withdrawn annually and 10 million acre-feet in water depleted might be expected. In contrast, a White House Drought Study Group (1977) estimated potential savings in water withdrawals by irrigated agriculture of 40 to 50 million acre-feet per year and about 8 million acre-feet per year in consumption through a comprehensive conservation program.[21] The importance of these figures is illustrated by considering that the average annual flow of the water-short Upper Colorado River Basin is less than 15 million acre-feet per year and that of the Missouri River Basin (the nation's largest) is about 52 million acre-feet annually.

The major barrier, however, to any irrigation conservation approaches, is outdated water rights laws passed a century ago to encourage settlement. Under the *doctrine of prior appropriation*, which applies in varying forms in most western states, the first owner to tap a river or stream can take as much water for "beneficial" purposes as his land can use. Thus, even though new irrigation techniques allow him to get along with much less water, the farmer has every incentive to use all the water he is historically entitled to or legally jeopardize his right to it, which would depress the value of his property. One solution would be to redefine *beneficial use* as the quantity that can be used efficiently on the land.

Land Management

Since forest- and rangeland occupy a third of the nation's land area, and forestland in particular receives more precipitation per acre than most other kinds of land, it follows that good forest and range management is important to good water management. The treatment and manipulation of the vegetative cover on a given area can either increase or decrease the yield and quality of water that flows from it. Appropriate silvicultural practices can increase the natural recharge of groundwater by slowing the rate of overland flow and increasing the infiltration rate. Such practices tend to maintain a more uniform flow of water from the headwaters of streams, providing a more dependable water supply for downstream users as well as reducing the potential for flooding.

Careful planning and implementation of the activities associated with land management can also minimize the amount of pollutants that enter lakes and streams. Such diverse activities as logging, road construction, cutting and burning of vegetation, use of pesticides and fertilizers, recreation, grazing, and off-vehicle use all are potential producers of some kind of pollution. When, where, and how they are done greatly influence the quality of water that flows from forest-and rangeland.

Much of this land is privately owned and in small holdings. Few of these owners have the necessary capital or technical expertise to plan or apply needed conservation measures. Because the benefits of such practices do not accrue specifically to the landowner but to society as a whole, public financial and technical assistance may be necessary.

Research has already produced much useful information about the management of land and water resources. Further work is needed, however, especially on techniques such as reducing consumptive use, managing forest- and rangeland to control pollution, reclaiming disturbed land, and identifying sources of, and controlling, acid rain.

Municipal and Industrial Conservation

On the municipal and industrial scene, large reductions in water use through applications of conservation measures are also possible. Savings of 20 percent or more are feasible by changing patterns of water use and developing plumbing codes that require installation of water-saving devices in new construction. Manufacturers nationwide use about 61 billion gallons a day, more than two thirds of which is used for cooling and condensing. Hence, the largest single savings is to stop a once-through-the-plant process and begin the internal recirculation of the cooling water. This fundamental change in tactic can bring about extraordinary variations in the volume of water used. Another critical advantage of the conserving and recycling techniques is that they make possible far more control over noxious wastes and chemicals (or even their recovery and reuse), so the water flow can be prevented from simply carrying them off into the nearest watercourse.

In addition, there is the relatively simple procedure of using for factory processes not the river's pristine flow but recycled water from the city's sewage treatment plant. Not all water needs to be at a standard fit for drinking to do its work. Partially treated water (for example, with the grit and sediment removed, as in primary treatment) can be used for the town's factory system. This is already happening in Kawasaki, in Japan, and near Naples, in Italy. As Barbara Ward concludes:

> Within such a division lies the germ of a new idea, at least for new settlements — to establish a dual system, providing two qualities of water: one meeting prescribed standards for drinking, cooking, bathing, and certain high-quality industrial needs; the other for general use in the factory or in domestic lavatories and garages, recycled through its own second-grade circuit.[22]

All of these various conservation efforts involve much more than just employing new technologies or even new modes of managing resources by farmers, foresters, and industrial officials. Basically, they all relate to that complex of water policy issues highlighted at the outset of this section. In light of such a serious gaggle of knotty issues, overlapping jurisdictions, and outmoded policies, it is necessary that our past achievements and failures in water policy be examined carefully and objectively in the context of the 1980s and beyond. Today's water-related problems simply require fundamental changes in water policy.

Roles of Federal, State, and Local Governments

Fundamental to the resolution of most critical water problems is the need for determining the appropriate roles to be played by federal, state, and local governments. Redefinition of the federal government's role in water resources planning and associated processes certainly merits consideration.

But it is at the state level where the most serious change is required. According to a 1980 report by the Water Resources Council, (WRC) state-federal cooperation is limited by the fact that only 29 states have clear legislative or administrative authority to conduct comprehensive water resources planning.[23] Even in the states with such authority, water quality and water quantity programs are often administered by separate, inadequately integrated government units. In only a few states, notably Delaware and Florida, are planning and management unified in a single agency. The WRC report stated that the lack of state legislative and administrative authority limits the states' ability to manage such serious problems as groundwater overdraft and pollution, floodplain management, erosion and sedimentation in surface waters, and drainage and dredging of wetlands.

State-federal cooperation is especially important to the solution of groundwater depletion and pollution problems. The EPA has worked with the states on a national groundwater strategy as a framework for state and federal action.

Granted, an effort to carefully delineate the division of federal, state, and local responsibility on the basis of today's needs and the relative opportunities that still exist for intrastate versus interstate development would entail considerable cost in legislative time, disputes, and political risk. Nevertheless, unless Congress resolves this issue, it is unlikely that significant progress will be made in solving the nation's critical water-related problems.

A CONCLUDING NOTE

Healthy rates of economic growth over the long run will only be achieved if that growth is built upon much more judicious management and use of the nation's natural resources. Natural resources — the ultimate supply factor — will act either as a serious constraint or as a vibrant, sustaining contributor to growth. The positive contribution will come about only if we as a nation make some broad-ranging investments in our resource base.

NOTES

CHAPTER 1

1. President Theodore Roosevelt, (Speech delivered at the National Governor's Conference, 1908).

2. Calculation by Harrison Brown, cited in John Holdren, "Technology, Environment, and Well Being: Some Critical Choices," in *Growth in America*, ed. Chester Cooper (Westport, Conn.: Greenwood Press, 1976), p. 95.

3. Preston Cloud, "Mineral Resources in Fact and Fancy," in *Toward a Steady State Economy*, ed. Herman E. Daly (San Francisco: W. H. Freeman, 1973), p. 6.

4. Arnold Toynbee, "After the Age of Affluence," *Skeptic*, July-August 1974, p. 38.

5. Barbara Ward, *Progress for a Small Planet* (New York: W. W. Norton, 1979), p. 266.

6. Alexis de Tocqueville, *Democracy in America*, trans. Henry Reeve (1835, 1840; reprint ed., London: Oxford University Press, 1952), pp. 343–44.

7. Denis Hayes, "Repairs, Reuse and Recycling-First Steps toward a Sustainable Society," Worldwatch Paper no. 23 (Washington, D.C.: Worldwatch Institute, September 1978), p. 38.

8. John Maynard Keynes, "Economic Possibilities for Our Grandchildren," in *Essays in Persuasion*, ed. J. M. Keynes (New York: St. Martins Press, 1930).

CHAPTER 2

1. U.S., Department of Agriculture (USDA), *Soil and Water Resource Conservation Act, 1980 Appraisal Part 1, Soil, Water, and Related Resources in the United States* (Washington, D.C.: USDA, 1981), pp. 49–50.

2. Council on Environmental Quality, *National Agricultural Lands Study* Final Report (Washington, D.C.: Government Printing Office, 1981), p. 25.

3. Ibid., Final Report, p. 25.

of the Carbon Dioxide Effects Research and Assessment Program (Springfield, Va.: National Technical Information Service, 1979).

16. National Research Council, Commission on Natural Resources, Board on Agriculture and Renewable Resources, and Committee on the Atmosphere and the Biosphere, *Atmosphere-Biosphere Interactions: Toward a Better Understanding of the Ecological Consequences of Fossil Fuel Combustion* (Washington, D.C.: National Academy Press, 1981), p. 3.

17. Ibid., p. 7.

18. National Academy of Sciences, Panel on Stratospheric Chemistry and Transport, *Stratospheric Ozone Depletion by Halocarbons: Chemistry and Transport* (Washington, D.C.: National Academy Press, 1979); and National Academy of Sciences, Committee on Impacts of Stratospheric Changes, *Protection against Depletion of Stratospheric Ozone by Chlorofluorocarbons* (Washington, D.C.: National Academy Press, 1979).

19. The statistics in this section come mainly from *Global 2000 Report*, vol. 1.

CHAPTER 4

1. Peter F. Drucker, "The Next American Work Force: Demographics and U.S. Economic Policy," *Commentary*, October 1981, p. 3.

2. Statistics from Forecasting International, Ltd., cited in "Jobs: Putting America Back to Work," *Newsweek*, October 18, 1982, p. 83.

CHAPTER 5

1. Harold Barnett and Chandler Morse, *Scarcity and Growth: The Economics of Natural Resource Availability* (Baltimore: Johns Hopkins University Press, 1963).

2. Nicholas Georgescu-Roegen, in *Scarcity and Growth Reconsidered*, ed. V. K. Smith (Baltimore: Johns Hopkins University Press, 1979), pp. 97–98.

3. James Tobin and William Nordhaus, *Economic Growth* (New York: Columbia University Press, 1972), p. 14.

4. Bertrand de Jouvenel, "A Letter to Walter Heller on the Inadequacy of Economics," mimeographed.

5. Edward F. Denison, *Accounting for United States Economic Growth, 1929–69* (Washington, D.C.: Brookings Institution, 1974).

6. W. Stanley Jevons, *The Theory of Political Economy*, 4th ed. (London: Macmillan, 1924), p. 21.

7. V. Kerry Smith, "The Evaluation of Natural Resource Adequacy: Elusive Quest or Frontier of Economic Analysis?" *Land Economics*, August 1980, p. 260.

8. Barnett and Morse. *Scarcity and Growth*, p. 11.

9. Harold Hotelling, "The Economics of Exhaustible Resources," *Journal of Political Economy* (1931): 137–75.

10. R.M. Solow, "The Economics of Resources and the Resources of Economics," *American Economic Review*, May 1974.

11. Talbot Page, *Conservation and Economic Efficiency* (Baltimore: Johns Hopkins University Press, 1977), p. 5

12. Barnett and Morse, *Scarcity and Growth*, p. 244.

CHAPTER 6

1. Harold Barnett and Chandler Morse, *Scarcity and Growth: The Economics of Natural Resource Availability* (Baltimore: Johns Hopkins University Press, 1963).

2. Harold J. Barnett, "Scarcity and Growth Revisited," in *Scarcity and Growth Reconsidered*, ed. V. K. Smith (Baltimore: Johns Hopkins University Press, 1979).

3. Pierre Crosson, "Long-run Costs of Production in American Agriculture," unpublished paper (Washington, D.C.: Resources for the Future, 1978); Manuel H. Johnson and Frederick W. Bell, "Resources and Scarcity: Are There Limits to Growth?" unpublished paper (Fairfax, Va.: George Mason University, n.d.); V. Kerry Smith, "Measuring Natural Resources Scarcity: Theory and Practice," *Journal of Environmental Economics and Management*, June 1978, pp. 150–71; idem, "Natural Resource Scarcity: A Statistical Analysis," *Review of Economics and Statistics*, August 1979, pp. 423–37.

4. V. Kerry Smith, "The Evaluation of Natural Resource Adequacy: Elusive Quest or Frontier of Economic Analysis," *Land Economics*, August 1980, p. 293.

5. Allen V. Kneese, "Energy Conservation Policies," *Natural Resources Journal*, October 1978, p. 822.

6. Cited in Herman E. Daly, *Steady State Economics* (San Francisco: W. H. Freeman, 1977), p. 43.

7. Talbot Page, *Conservation and Economic Efficiency* (Baltimore: Johns Hopkins University Press, 1977), p. 9.

8. Aldo Leopold, *A Sand Country Almanac* (New York: Oxford University Press, 1949), p. 93.

9. Lewis C. Gray, "Economic Possibilities of Conservation," *Quarterly Journal of Economics*, 1913, p. 499.

10. Page, *Conservation and Economic Efficiency*, p. 200.

11. Ibid., p. 250; James Doilney, "Equity, Efficiency, and Intertemporal Resource Allocation Decisions" (Ph.D. diss., University of Maryland, 1974), chap. 3, p. 13.

12. Joan Robinson, "The Second Crisis of Economic Theory," *American Economic Review*, May 1972, p. 10.

CHAPTER 7

1. Alfred E. Kahn, "Environmental Values Are Economic," *Challenge*, May-June 1979, p. 67.

2. Alfred Marshall, *Principles of Economics* (London: Macmillan, 1890), p. 258.

3. W. Stanley Jevons, *The Theory of Political Economy*, 4th ed. (London: Macmillan, 1924).

4. Nicholas Georgescu-Roegen, "Energy and Economic Myths," *Southern Economic Journal*, January 1975.

5. Carl H. Madden, *Clash of Culture: Management in an Age of Changing Values* (Washington, D.C.: National Planning Association, 1972), p. 20.

6. Georgescu-Roegen, "Energy and Economic Myths," p. 353.

7. Stephen E. Harris, *The Death of Capital* (New York: Pantheon Books, 1978), p. 4.

8. Marshall, *Principles of Economics*, p. 14.

9. Cited in Richard B. Gregg, *A Philosophy of Indian Economic Development* (Ahmedabad, India: Narajivan Publishing House, 1958).

10. The discussion of three types of values is drawn from Edward G. Farnworth, Thomas H. Tidrick, Carl F. Jordan, and Webb M. Smathers, "The Value of Natural Ecosystems: An Economic and Ecological Framework," *Environmental Conservation*, Winter 1981, pp. 275–282.

11. Nicholas Georgescu-Roegen, *The Entropy Law and the Economic Process* (Cambridge: Harvard University Press, 1971) p. 276.

12. Herman E. Daly, "The Steady State Economy: What, Why and How?" unpublished paper (Baton Rouge: Louisiana State University), p. 5.

13. Georgescu-Roegen, *The Entropy Law and the Economic Process* pp. 281–82.

14. Ibid., p. 282.

15. Ibid., p. 278.

16. Robert M. Solow, "Is the End of the World at Hand?" *Challenge,* March–April 1973.

17. Nicholas Georgescu-Roegen, "Energy, Matter and Economic Valuation: Where Do We Stand?" in *Energetic and Ecological Economics,* ed. A. Umana and Herman E. Daly, 1980.

18. Herman E. Daly, *Steady-State Economics* (San Francisco: W. H. Freeman and Company, 1977), p. 23.

19. Ibid.

20. Ibid., pp. 172–73.

21. Nicholas Georgescu-Roegen, "Economics and Mankind's Ecological Problem," in *The Limits to Growth,* U.S. Economic Growth from 1976–1986: Prospects, Problems and Patterns, vol. 7 (Washington, D.C.: Government Printing Office, 1976).

CHAPTER 8

1. Gifford Pinchot quotes cited in Allen V. Kneese, "Energy Conservation Policies," *Natural Resources Journal,* October 1978, p. 815.

2. U.S., Resource Conservation Committee, *Choices for Conservation* (Washington, D.C.: Environmental Protection Agency, July 1979), p. 1.

3. Willis W. Harman, *An Incomplete Guide to the Future* (San Francisco: San Francisco Book Company, 1976), p. 47.

4. Daniel Yankelovich and Bernard Lefkowitz, "The Public Debate about Growth," in *The Management of Sustainable Growth,* ed. Harlan Cleveland (New York: Pergamon Press, 1981).

5. Continental Group, "Economic Growth Is Compatible with Environmental Preservation," *Financier,* December 1982, pp. 44–45.

6. Theodore Roosevelt quoted in Roderick Nash, *The American Environment: Readings in the History of Conservation* (Menlo Park, California: Addison-Wesley, 1968), p. 50.

7. Roger W. Sant, "Cutting Energy Costs," *Environment,* May 1980, pp. 19–20.

8. *The Global 2000 Report to the President:Entering the 21st Century,* Council on Environmental Quality and the Department of State (Washington, D.C.: Government Printing Office, 1980).

CHAPTER 9

1. Arthur Miller, *Death of a Salesman* (New York: Viking Press, 1949).

2. Denis Hayes, "Repairs, Reuse and Recycling—First Steps toward a Sustainable Society," Worldwatch paper no. 23 (Washington, D.C.: Worldwatch, September 1978); p. 24.

3. A. G. Chynoweth, "Materials Conservation: A Technologist's Viewpoint," *Challenge,* January-February 1976, p. 39.

4. F. Lynn, "An Investigation of the Rates of Development and Diffusion of Technology in Our Modern Industrial Society," in *Report of the National Commission on Technology, Automation, and Economic Progress* (Washington, D.C.: Government Printing Office, 1966).

5. L. Nasbeth and G. F. Ray, *The Diffusion of New Industrial Processes: An International Study* (New York: Cambridge University Press, 1974).

6. P. B. Humphrey and J. R. Moroney, "Substitution Among Capital, Labor, and Natural Resources Products in American Manufacturing," *Journal of Political Economy,* February 1975.

7. This discussion of waste exchange draws on R. G. W. Laughlin, "Waste Exchange: Industry's Disposal Alternative," *Waste Age,* November 1980, pp. 40–41.

8. Cited in "Fighting Over Scraps: Steel Mills vs. Recyclers," *Washington Post,* September 4, 1977.

9. Herman E. Daly, Introduction to *Toward a Steady State Economy,* ed. H. Daly (San Francisco: W. H. Freeman, 1973), p. 16.

10. Zimmerman, "Institutional and Political Aspects of Waste Recycling and Management," unpublished paper (May 1974).

11. U.S., Treasury Department, *Federal Tax Policy and Recycling of Solid Waste Materials* (Washington, D.C.: Government Printing Office, 1979).

12. Talbot Page, *Conservation and Economic Efficiency* (Baltimore: Johns Hopkins University Press, 1977), p. 210.

13. Betsy Goggin and Michele Hodak, "Co-Disposal: A New Technology," *EPA Journal,* September 1979, pp. 20–21.

14. Hayes, "Repairs," p. 31.

CHAPTER 10

1. Harlan Cleveland and Alexander King, "The Renewable Way of Life," *Futurist,* April 1980, pp. 47–80.

2. *The Global 2000 Report to the President:Entering the 21st Century,* Council on Environmental Quality and the Department of State (Washington, D.C.: Government Printing Office, 1981).

3. Cleveland and King, "Renewable Way," p. 52.

4. "Investing for Prosperity," The Resources Agency, State of California, January 1981.

5. Lewis J. Perleman, "The Ark Plan: A Renewable-Resources Trust Fund for the United States," *Energy, Economics and the Environment,* ed. Gregory A. Daneke (Lexington, Mass.: D.C. Heath, 1982), pp. 259–60, 263–64.

6. U.S., Office of Technology Assessment, *Energy from Biological Processes,* Summary (Washington, D.C.: Office of Technology Assessment, 1980), p. 7.

7. David Pimentel, Mary Ann Moran, Sarah Fast, Georg Weber, Robert Bukantis, Lisa Balliett, Peter Boveng, Cutler Cleveland, Sally Hindman, Martin Young, "Biomass Energy from Crop and Forest Residues," *Science,* June 1981, pp. 1110–1115.

8. Office of Technology Assessment, *Energy from Biological Processes,* p. 7.

9. Ibid., vol. 2, p. 59.

10. Reported in *Synfuels Week,* September 15, 1980.

11. Office of Technology Assessment, *Energy from Biological Processes,* Summary, p. 18.

12. Ibid., vol. 2, pp. 45–46.

13. Ibid., vol. 2, p. 46.

14. Stephen E. Plotkin, "Energy from Biomass," *Environment,* November 1980, p. 40.

15. Leonard Rodberg and Meg Schachter, *State Conservation and Solar Energy Tax Programs: Incentives or Windfalls* (Washington, D.C.: Council of State Planning Agencies, 1980), p. 7.

16. *Governor's Policy Initiatives* (Washington, D.C.: National Governors' Association, Center for Policy Research, 1980), p. 16.

17. Loren Wilkinson, ed. *Earthkeeping* (Grand Rapids, Michigan: William B. Eerdmans, 1980) p. 16.

18. Cited in Barbara Ward, *Progress for a Small Planet* (New York: W. W. Norton, 1979), p. 111.

19. Barry Commoner, *The Poverty of Power* (New York: Knopf, 1977), p. 163.

20. Forest Industries Council, *Forest Productivity Report,* (Washington, D.C.: National Forests Products Association, 1980), p. 46.

21. Cited in Warren Viessman, Jr., "Water—Supply and Demand, Issues and Trends," Background paper for the National Conference on Renewable Natural Resources, sponsored by the American Forestry Association, Washington, D.C., November 30-December 3, 1980, p. 40.

22. Ward, *Progress for a Small Planet,* p. 86.

23. U.S., Water Resources Council, *State of the States: Water Resources Planning and Management* (Washington, D.C.: Government Printing Office, 1980), p. II-2.

INDEX

ABOUT THE AUTHOR

Robert D. Hamrin has had extensive academic, research, consulting, and Legislative as well as Executive Branch government experience in economic policy. He has served as economic advisor to Senator Gary Hart since early 1982. He has been a college teacher; a staff economist with the Joint Economic Committee of Congress, where he served as director of the twelve-volume study series *U.S. Economic Growth from 1976-1986: Prospects, Problems, and Patterns*; a Fellow of the Rockefeller Foundation; a professional staff member of the President's Commission for a National Agenda for the Eighties under the Carter Administration; and Senior Policy Economist and Director of the Benefits Group at the U.S. Environmental Protection Agency.

His professional activities outside his employment have covered a wide and diverse spectrum. He has lectured frequently at colleges and universities and for organizations ranging from the World Future Society to the Chinese Ministry of Foreign Affairs and the Chinese Academy of Social Sciences. He has been a consultant to such diverse organizations as the Council on Environmental Quality, Department of State, Club of Rome and the Business Roundtable. He has published three previous books, three reports and numerous articles in books and journals.

Dr. Hamrin received his B.A. in Economics and Mathematics (Phi Beta Kappa) from St. Olaf College and his Ph.D in economics from the University of Wisconsin. He is married and the father of three children.